DISCARD

ABORTION DECISIONS
OF THE UNITED STATES
SUPREME COURT

THE 1970'S

MAUREEN HARRISON & STEVE GILBERT
EDITORS

ABORTION DECISIONS SERIES

EXCELLENT BOOKS
BEVERLY HILLS, CALIFORNIA

EXCELLENT BOOKS
Post Office Box 7121
Beverly Hills, CA 90212-7121

Publisher's Cataloging in Publication Data

Abortion Decisions of the United States Supreme Court: The 1970's/
 Maureen Harrison, Steve Gilbert, editors.
 p. cm. - (Abortion Decisions Series)
 Bibliography: p.
 Includes Index.
 1. Abortion - United States, 2. Abortion - Political Aspects -
 United States, 3. Abortion - Government Policy, 4. Abortion -
 Law and Legislation, 5. United States Supreme Court
 I. Title. II. Harrison, Maureen. III. Gilbert, Steve.
 IV. Series: Abortion Decisions.
 HQ767.5.U5 H24 1993 LC 92-75836
 363.4'6 - dc20

ISBN 0-9628014-4-5

Introduction

"If any person shall designedly administer to a pregnant woman or knowingly procure to be administered with her consent any drug or medicine, or shall shall use towards her any violence or means whatever externally or internally applied, and thereby procure an abortion, he shall be confined in the penitentiary not less than two nor more than five years; if it be done without her consent, the punishment shall be doubled. By 'abortion' is meant that the life of the fetus or embryo shall be destroyed in the woman's womb or that a premature birth thereof be caused."

Article 1191, Texas Penal Code (1857)

"Since my pregnancy I have experienced difficulty in securing employment. Each month I am barely able to make ends meet. Consequently I cannot afford to travel to another jurisdiction in order to secure a legal abortion. I understand that there are competent licensed physicians in Dallas County who do perform apparently illegal abortions, but I have never been able to afford their services. I fear that my very life would be endangered if I submitted to an abortion which I could afford. I believe that the enforcement of the Texas Abortion Laws against licensed physicians had forced me into the dilemma of electing whether to bear an unwanted child or to risk my life submitting to an abortion at the hands of unqualified personnel outside of clinical settings."

Excerpted from the affidavit of Jane Roe,
in the case of *Roe v. Wade*

If you are passionately pro-life, January 22, 1973 marks the start of a slaughter of the innocents. If you are fervently pro-choice, January 22, 1973 marks the end of unwanted pregnancies and back alley abortions. January 22, 1973 marks, in fact, the day the United States Supreme Court issued the landmark abortion decision, *Roe v. Wade.* On that day twenty years ago the Court, voting 7-2, struck down as unconstitutional the Texas, and, by extension, all similar state abortion statutes. The legal war of words that has resulted in challenges to and defenses of the right of women to choose abortion is the reason for this series.

Twenty-one times in twenty years the United States Supreme Court has issued major abortion decisions. The divisions of opinion over abortion in this country are reflected in the divisions of opinion within the Court. The majority and minority opinions of the Justices echo the national debate, and sometimes the national shouting match, now twenty years old. This book covers the first eight major decisions issued by the Court in the decade of the 1970's.

For the first time all these major decisions are presented in plain English for the general reader. In each of these carefully edited versions of the official texts issued by the Supreme Court, the editors have tried to decipher the Court's legalese without damaging or diminishing the original decision. Edited out are alpha-numeric legal citations, micro print footnotes, and wordy wrangles over points of procedure. Edited in [in brackets] are definitions [*stare decisis* = leave past decisions undisturbed], translations [*certiorari* = the decision of the Court to review a case], identifications [Appellant = Roe, Appellee = Wade], and explanations [where the case originated, how it got before the court, and who the major parties were]. You will find in this book the majority opinion of the Court as expressed by the Justice chosen to speak for the Court. All concurring and dissenting opinions of the Justices are included. A complete copy of the United States Constitution, to which all the decisions refer, follows the abortion decisions.

The Supreme Court of the United States is the court of final appeal for all legal controversies arising in the federal courts and all federal issues arising in the state courts. Only the Court has the authority to construct and interpret the meaning of the Constitution. "We are not final," wrote Justice Robert Jackson, "because we are infallible, but we are infallible because we are final." From 1857's Slavery Decision in *Dred Scott* to 1973's Abortion Decision in *Roe v. Wade*, controversy and the Court have been longtime companions.

Justice Oliver Wendell Holmes wrote: "[The Constitution] is made for people of fundamentally differing views, and the accident of our finding certain opinions natural and familiar or novel and even shocking ought not to conclude our judgment upon the question whether statutes embodying them conflict with the United States Constitution."

Those "fundamentally differing opinions" are evident in the first eight major abortion decisions issued in the 1970's:

In 1973's *Roe v. Wade* at issue is the constitutionality of the Texas, and, by extension, all similar state criminal abortion laws. The parties are Jane Roe, the pseudonym of an unmarried, pregnant indigent woman, and Henry Wade, Dallas, Texas District Attorney. The majority decision of the Court is by Justice Harry Blackmun.

In 1973's *Doe v. Bolton*, the companion case of *Roe v. Wade*, at issue is the constitutionality of the Georgia, and, by extension, all similar state criminal abortion laws. The parties are Mary Doe, the pseudonym of a married, pregnant, indigent woman, and Arthur Bolton, Georgia Attorney General. The majority decision of the Court is by Justice Harry Blackmun.

In 1976's *Planned Parenthood v. Danforth* at issue is the constitutionality of the Missouri abortion law, the first major challenge to 1973's *Roe* and *Doe* Abortion Decisions. The parties are Planned Parenthood of Central Missouri and John Danforth, Missouri Attorney General. The majority decision of the Court is by Justice Harry Blackmun.

In 1977's *Beal v. Doe* at issue is the constitutionality of publicly-funded Medicaid abortions in Pennsylvania hospitals. The parties are Frank Beal, Secretary, Pennsylvania Department of Welfare, and Ann Doe, the pseudonym of an indigent. The majority decision of the Court is by Justice Lewis Powell.

In 1977's *Maher v. Roe*, the companion case to *Beal v. Doe*, at issue is publicly-funded Medicaid abortions in Connecticut hospitals. The parties are Edward Maher, Connecticut Commissioner of Social Services, and Susan Roe, the pseudonym of an indigent. The majority decision of the Court is by Justice Lewis Powell.

In 1977's *Poelker v. Doe* at issue is the constitutionality of an official city policy not to perform abortions in city hospitals. The parties are John Poelker, Mayor, St. Louis, Missouri, and Jane Doe, the pseudonym of an indigent. The majority decision of the Court is Per Curiam [by the Court].

In 1979's *Colautti v. Franklin* at issue is the constitutionality of the Pennsylvania abortion law, the second major challenge to 1973's *Roe* and *Doe* Abortion Decisions. The parties are Aldo Colautti, Secretary, Pennsylvania Department of Welfare, and John Franklin, Director, Planned Parenthood of Southeastern Pennsylvania. The majority decision of the Court is by Justice Harry Blackmun.

In 1979's *Bellotti v. Baird* at issue is Massachusetts requirements for parental consent for a minors abortion. The parties are Francis Bellotti, Massachusetts Attorney General and William Baird, Director, Parents Aid Society. The majority decision of the Court is by Justice Lewis Powell.

The tremendous impact of these first eight decisions can be measured, quantitatively, by statistics on abortion collected by the United States Government throughout the decade of the 1970's:

744,600 legal abortions were performed on women ages 15 through 44 in 1973 - 244,000 on teenagers, 370,200 on women in their twenties, 113,600 on women in their thirties, and 16,800 on women forty and over.

898,600 legal abortions were performed on women ages 15 through 44 in 1974 - 291,700 on teenagers, 449,300 on women in their twenties, 138,600 on women in their thirties, and 19,000 on women forty and over.

1,034,200 legal abortions were performed on women ages 15 through 44 in 1975. 340,200 on teenagers, 520,500 on women in their twenties, 152,900 on women in their thirties, and 20,500 on women forty and over.

1,179,300 legal abortions were performed on women ages

15 through 44 in 1976 - 378,500 on teenagers, 612,800 on women in their twenties, 152,900 on women in their thirties, and 20,500 on women forty and over.

1,316,700 legal abortions were performed on women ages 15 through 44 in 1977 - 412,300 on teenagers, 696,400 on women in their twenties, 186,100 on women in their thirties, and 22,000 on women forty and over.

1,409,600 legal abortions were performed on women ages 15 through 44 in 1978 - 433,900 on teenagers, 755,400 on women in their twenties, 199,600 on women in their thirties, and 20,700 on women forty and over.

1,497,700 legal abortions were performed on women ages 15 through 44 in 1979 - 460,800 on teenagers, 809,900 on women in their twenties, 207,100 on women in their thirties, and 19,900 on women forty and over.

Judge Learned Hand wrote: "The language of the law must not be foreign to the ears of those who are to obey it." This is the first of three volumes that will reproduce in readable form the abortion decisions of the United States Supreme Court. We have tried as hard as we could, as Judge Hand urged us, to make these decision less foreign to your ears.

M.H. & S.G.

TABLE OF CONTENTS

"One's philosophy, one's experiences, one's exposure to the raw edges of human existence, one's religious training, one's attitudes toward life and family and their values, and the moral standards one establishes and seeks to observe, are all likely to influence and to color one's thinking and conclusions about abortion."

Justice Harry Blackmun

" . . . [T]he Court's opinion will accomplish the seemingly impossible feat of leaving this area of the law more confused than it found it."

Justice William Rehnquist

"It would be physically and emotionally damaging to Doe to bring a child into her poor "fatherless" family. . . . [A]dvances in medicine and medical techniques have made it safer for a woman to have a medically induced abortion than for her to bear a child."

Justice Harry Blackmun

PLANNED PARENTHOOD v. DANFORTH
75

"[T]he State does not have the constitutional authority to give a third party an absolute, and possibly arbitrary, veto over the decision of the physician and his patient to terminate the patient's pregnancy, regardless of the reason for withholding the consent."

Justice Harry Blackmun

BEAL v. DOE
105

"The Court's construction can only result as a practical matter in forcing penniless pregnant women to have children they would not have borne if the State had not weighted the scales to make their choice to have abortions substantially more onerous. . ."

Justice William Brennan

MAHER v. ROE
121

"*Roe* did not declare an unqualified 'constitutional right to an abortion.' . . . Rather, the right protects the woman from unduly burdensome interference with her freedom to decide whether to terminate her pregnancy. It implies no limitation on the authority of a State to make a value judgment favoring childbirth over abortion, and to implement that judgment by the allocation of public funds."

Justice Lewis Powell

ABOUT THE EDITORS
OF THE ABORTION DECISIONS SERIES

MAUREEN HARRISON is a textbook editor and a
member of the Supreme Court Historical Society

STEVE GILBERT is a law librarian and a member of the
American Association of Law Libraries and the
American Bar Association

Harrison & Gilbert are also the editors of:

THE LANDMARK DECISIONS SERIES

THE AMERICANS WITH DISABILITIES ACT
HANDBOOK

THE ABORTION LAW SOURCEBOOK

ROE v. WADE

EXCERPTS

"One's philosophy, one's experiences, one's exposure to the raw edges of human existence, one's religious training, one's attitudes toward life and family and their values, and the moral standards one establishes and seeks to observe, are all likely to influence and to color one's thinking and conclusions about abortion."

Justice Harry Blackmun

"Plainly, the Court today rejects any claim that the Constitution requires abortion on demand."

Chief Justice Warren Burger

" . . . [T]he Court's opinion will accomplish the seemingly impossible feat of leaving this area of the law more confused than it found it."

Justice William Rehnquist

In Brief

Question:	Is the Texas criminal abortion law constitutional?
Lower Court:	U.S. District Court, Northern Texas
Law:	Texas Penal Code, Article 1196
Parties:	Jane Roe, pseudonym of Norma Mc Corvey Henry Wade, Dallas District Attorney
Counsel:	For Roe: Sara R. Weddington For Wade: Jay Floyd, Robert Flowers
Arguments:	December 13, 1971; October 11, 1972
Decision:	January 22, 1973
Majority:	Chief Justice Burger, Justices Douglas, Brennan, Stewart, Marshall, Blackmun, Powell
Minority:	Justices White, Rehquist
Decision by:	Justice Blackmun (p. 5)
Concurrences:	Chief Justice Burger (p. 34) Justice Douglas (p. 35) Justice Stewart (p. 44)
Dissents:	Justice White (p. 47) Justice Rehnquist (p. 49)
Offical Text:	U.S. Reports, Vol. 410, page 113
Lower Court:	Federal Supplement, Vol. 314, page 1217

THE ROE COURT

Chief Justice Warren Burger
Appointed 1969 by Richard M. Nixon

Associate Justice William O. Douglas
Appointed 1939 by Franklin D. Roosevelt

Associate Justice William Brennan
Appointed 1956 by Dwight D. Eisenhower

Associate Justice Potter Stewart
Appointed 1958 by Dwight D. Eisenhower

Associate Justice Byron White
Appointed 1962 by John F. Kennedy

Associate Justice Thurgood Marshall
Appointed 1967 by Lyndon B. Johnson

Associate Justice Harry Blackmun
Appointed 1970 by Richard M. Nixon

Associate Justice Lewis Powell
Appointed 1972 by Richard M. Nixon

Associate Justice William Rehnquist
Appointed 1971 by Richard M. Nixon

ROE v. WADE

January 22, 1973

JUSTICE HARRY BLACKMUN: This Texas federal appeal . . . present[s] constitutional challenges to state criminal abortion legislation. The Texas statutes under attack here are typical of those that have been in effect in many States for approximately a century. . . .

We forthwith acknowledge our awareness of the sensitive and emotional nature of the abortion controversy, of the vigorous opposing views, even among physicians, and of the deep and seemingly absolute convictions that the subject inspires. One's philosophy, one's experiences, one's exposure to the raw edges of human existence, one's religious training, one's attitudes toward life and family and their values, and the moral standards one establishes and seeks to observe, are all likely to influence and to color one's thinking and conclusions about abortion.

. . . . "[The Constitution] is made for people of fundamentally differing views, and the accident of our finding certain opinions natural and familiar or novel and even shocking ought not to conclude our judgment upon the question whether statutes embodying them conflict with the Constitution of the United States."

The Texas statutes that concern us here . . . make it a crime to "procure an abortion," . . . or to attempt one, except with respect to "an abortion procured or attempted by medical advice for the purpose of saving the life of the mother." Similar statutes are in existence in a majority of the States.

Texas first enacted a criminal abortion statute in 1854. This was soon modified [in 1857, 1866, 1879, and 1911] into language that has remained substantially unchanged to the present time. The final article in each of these compilations provided the same exception . . . for an abortion by "medical advice for the purpose of saving the life of the mother."

Jane Roe [the name is a pseudonym], a single woman who was residing in Dallas County, Texas, instituted this federal action in March 1970 against the District Attorney of the county. She sought a declaratory judgment [a conclusive, binding statement by the court] that the Texas criminal abortion statutes were unconstitutional . . . and an injunction [an order from the court] restraining [preventing] the defendant [the District Attorney] from enforcing the statutes.

Roe [claimed] that she was unmarried and pregnant; that she wished to terminate her pregnancy by an abortion "performed by a competent, licensed physician, under safe, clinical conditions"; that she was unable to get a "legal" abortion in Texas because her life did not appear to be threatened by the continuation of her pregnancy; and that she could not afford to travel to another jurisdiction in order to secure a legal abortion under safe conditions. She claimed that the Texas statutes were unconstitutionally vague and that they abridged her right of personal privacy, protected by the First, Fourth, Fifth, Ninth, and Fourteenth Amendments. By an amendment to her complaint Roe purported to sue "on behalf of herself and all other women" similarly situated.

. . . . Despite the use of the pseudonym, no suggestion is made that Roe is a fictitious person. For purposes of her case, we accept as true, and as established, her existence; her pregnant state, as of the inception of her suit in March 1970 and as late as May 21 of that year when she filed an alias affidavit with the District Court; and her inability to obtain a legal abortion in Texas.

Viewing Roe's case as of the time of its filing and thereafter until as late as May, there can be little dispute that it then presented a case or controversy and that . . . she, as a pregnant single woman thwarted by the Texas criminal abortion laws, had [the legal right] to challenge those statutes. . . .

[Wade] notes, however, that the record does not disclose that Roe was pregnant at the time of the District Court hearing on May 22, 1970, or on the following June 17 when the court's opinion and judgment were filed. And he suggests that Roe's case must now be moot [no longer in controversy] because she . . . [is] no longer subject to any 1970 pregnancy.

The usual rule in federal cases is that an actual controversy must exist at stages of appellate . . . review, and not simply at the date the action is initiated.

But when, as here, pregnancy is a significant fact in the litigation, the normal 266-day human gestation period is so short that the pregnancy will come to term before the usual appellate process is complete. If that termination makes a case moot, pregnancy litigation seldom will survive much beyond the trial stage, and appellate review will be effectively denied. Our law should not be that rigid. Pregnancy often comes more than once to the same woman, and in the general population, if man is to survive, it will always be with us. Pregnancy provides a classic justification for a conclusion of nonmootness. It truly could be "capable of repetition, yet evading review."

We, therefore, agree with the District Court that Jane Roe had [the right] to undertake this litigation, that she presented a justiciable controversy, and that the termination of her 1970 pregnancy has not rendered her case moot.

. . . . The principal thrust of appellant's attack on the Texas statutes is that they improperly invade a right, said to be possessed by the pregnant woman, to choose to terminate her pregnancy. [Roe claims] this right in the concept of personal "liberty" embodied in the Fourteenth Amendment's Due Process Clause; or in personal, marital, familial, and sexual privacy said to be protected by the Bill of Rights or its penumbras; or among those rights reserved to the people by the Ninth Amendment. Before addressing this claim, we feel it desirable briefly to survey, in several aspects, the history of abortion, for such insight as that history may afford us, and then to examine the state purposes and interests behind the criminal abortion laws.

It perhaps is not generally appreciated that the restrictive criminal abortion laws in effect in a majority of States today are of relatively recent vintage. Those laws, generally proscribing [prohibiting] abortion or its attempt at any time during pregnancy except when necessary to preserve the pregnant woman's life, are not of ancient or even of common-law origin. Instead, they derive from statutory [legislative] changes effected, for the most part, in the latter half of the 19th century.

1. Ancient attitudes. These are not capable of precise determination. We are told that at the time of the Persian

Empire abortifacients were known and that criminal abortions were severely punished. We are also told, however, that abortion was practiced in Greek times as well as in the Roman Era, and that "it was resorted to without scruple." The Ephesian, Soranos, often described as the greatest of the ancient gynecologists, appears to have been generally opposed to Rome's prevailing free-abortion practices. He found it necessary to think first of the life of the mother, and he resorted to abortion when, upon this standard, he felt the procedure advisable. Greek and Roman law afforded little protection to the unborn. If abortion was prosecuted in some places, it seems to have been based on a concept of a violation of the father's right to his offspring. Ancient religion did not bar abortion.

2. The Hippocratic Oath. What then of the famous Oath that has stood so long as the ethical guide of the medical profession and that bears the name of the great Greek, who has been described as the Father of Medicine, the "wisest and the greatest practitioner of his art," and the "most important and most complete medical personality of antiquity," who dominated the medical schools of his time, and who typified the sum of the medical knowledge of the past? The Oath varies somewhat according to the particular translation, but in any translation the content is clear: "I will give no deadly medicine to anyone if asked, nor suggest any such counsel; and in like manner I will not give to a woman a pessary to produce abortion," or "I will neither give a deadly drug to anybody if asked for it, nor will I make a suggestion to this effect. Similarly, I will not give to a woman an abortive remedy."

Although the Oath is not mentioned in any of the principal briefs in this case . . . , it represents the apex of the development of strict ethical concepts in medicine, and its

influence endures to this day. Why did not the authority
of Hippocrates dissuade abortion practice in his time and
that of Rome? The late Dr. Edelstein provides us with a
theory: The Oath was not uncontested even in Hippocrates' day; only the Pythagorean school of philosophers
frowned upon the related act of suicide. Most Greek
thinkers, on the other hand, commended abortion, at least
prior to viability. For the Pythagoreans, however, it was a
matter of dogma. For them the embryo was animate from
the moment of conception, and abortion meant destruction of a living being. The abortion clause of the Oath,
therefore, "echoes Pythagorean doctrines," and "[i]n no
other stratum of Greek opinion were such views held or
proposed in the same spirit of uncompromising austerity."

Dr. Edelstein then concludes that the Oath originated in a
group representing only a small segment of Greek opinion
and that it certainly was not accepted by all ancient physicians. He points out that medical writings down to Galen
(A.D. 130-200) "give evidence of the violation of almost
every one of its injunctions." But with the end of antiquity a decided change took place. Resistance against suicide
and against abortion became common. The Oath came to
be popular. The emerging teachings of Christianity were
in agreement with the Pythagorean ethic. The Oath
"became the nucleus of all medical ethics" and "was ap-
plauded as the embodiment of truth." Thus, suggests Dr.
Edelstein, it is "a Pythagorean manifesto and not the expression of an absolute standard of medical conduct."

This, it seems to us, is a satisfactory and acceptable expla-
nation of the Hippocratic Oath's apparent rigidity. It enables us to understand, in historical context, a long-
accepted and revered statement of medical ethics.

3. The common law. It is undisputed that at common law [court decisions], abortion performed *before* "quickening" - the first recognizable movement of the fetus in utero, appearing usually from the 16th to the 18th week of pregnancy - was not an indictable offense. The absence of a common-law crime for pre-quickening abortion appears to have developed from a confluence of earlier philosophical, theological, and civil and canon law concepts of when life begins. These disciplines variously approached the question in terms of the point at which the embryo or fetus became "formed" or recognizably human, or in terms of when a "person" came into being, that is, infused with a "soul" or "animated." A loose consensus evolved in early English law that these events occurred at some point between conception and live birth. This was "mediate animation." Although Christian theology and the canon law came to fix the point of animation at 40 days for a male and 80 days for a female, a view that persisted until the 19th century, there was otherwise little agreement about the precise time of formation or animation. There was agreement, however, that prior to this point the fetus was to be regarded as part of the mother, and its destruction, therefore, was not homicide. Due to continued uncertainty about the precise time when animation occurred, to the lack of any empirical basis for the 40-80-day view, and perhaps to Aquinas' definition of movement as one of the two first principles of life, Bracton focused upon quickening as the critical point. The significance of quickening was echoed by later common-law scholars and found its way into the received [accepted] common law in this country.

Whether abortion of a *quick* fetus was a felony at common law, or even a lesser crime, is still disputed. Bracton, writing early in the 13th century, thought it homicide.

But the later and predominant view, following the great common-law scholars, has been that it was, at most, a lesser offense. In a frequently cited passage, Coke took the position that abortion of a woman "quick with childe" is "a great misprision [an undefined crime], and no murder." Blackstone followed, saying that while abortion after quickening had once been considered manslaughter (though not murder), "modern law" took a less severe view. A recent review of the common-law precedents argues, however, that those precedents contradict Coke and that even post-quickening abortion was never established as a common-law crime. This is of some importance because while most American courts ruled, in holding [actual decision] or dictum [observations made in the decision], that abortion of an unquickened fetus was not criminal under their received common law, others followed Coke in stating that abortion of a quick fetus was a "misprision," a term they translated to mean "misdemeanor." That their reliance on Coke on this aspect of the law was uncritical and, apparently in all the reported cases, dictum (due probably to the paucity of common-law prosecutions for post-quickening abortion), makes it now appear doubtful that abortion was ever firmly established as a common-law crime even with respect to the destruction of a quick fetus.

4. The English statutory law. England's first criminal abortion statute, Lord Ellenborough's Act, came in 1803. It made abortion of a quick fetus ... a capital crime, but ... it provided lesser penalties for the felony of abortion before quickening, and thus preserved the "quickening" distinction. This contrast was continued in the general revision of 1828. It disappeared, however, together with the death penalty, in 1837, and did not reappear in the Offenses Against the Person Act of 1861 that formed the

core of English anti-abortion law until the liberalizing reforms of 1967. In 1929, the Infant Life (Preservation) Act came into being. Its emphasis was upon the destruction of "the life of a child capable of being born alive." It made a willful act performed with the necessary intent a felony. It contained a proviso that one was not to be found guilty of the offense "unless it is proved that the act which caused the death of the child was not done in good faith for the purpose only of preserving the life of the mother."

A seemingly notable development in the English law was the case of *Rex v. Bourne*. This case apparently answered in the affirmative the question whether an abortion necessary to preserve the life of the pregnant woman was excepted from the criminal penalties of the 1861 Act. In his instructions to the jury, Judge Macnaghten referred to the 1929 Act, and observed that that Act related to "the case where a child is killed by a wilful act at the time when it is being delivered in the ordinary course of nature." He concluded that the 1861 Act's use of the word "unlawfully," imported the same meaning expressed by the specific proviso in the 1929 Act, even though there was no mention of preserving the mother's life in the 1861 Act. He then construed the phrase "preserving the life of the mother" broadly, that is, "in a reasonable sense," to include a serious and permanent threat to the mother's *health*, and instructed the jury to acquit Dr. Bourne if it found he had acted in a good-faith belief that the abortion was necessary for this purpose. The jury did acquit.

Recently, Parliament enacted a new abortion law. This is the Abortion Act of 1967. The Act permits a licensed physician to perform an abortion where two other licensed physicians agree (a) "that the continuance of the pregnancy would involve risk to the life of the pregnant woman, or of injury to the physical or mental health of the pregnant woman or any existing children of her family, greater than if the pregnancy were terminated," or (b) "that there is a substantial risk that if the child were born it would suffer from such physical or mental abnormalities as to be seriously handicapped." The Act also provides that, in making this determination, "account may be taken of the pregnant woman's actual or reasonably foreseeable environment." It also permits a physician, without the concurrence of others, to terminate a pregnancy where he is of the good-faith opinion that the abortion "is immediately necessary to save the life or to prevent grave permanent injury to the physical or mental health of the pregnant woman."

5. The American law. In this country, the law in effect in all but a few States until mid-19th century was the pre-existing English common law. Connecticut, the first State to enact abortion legislation, adopted in 1821 that part of Lord Ellenborough's Act that related to a woman "quick with child." The death penalty was not imposed. Abortion before quickening was made a crime in that State only in 1860. In 1828, New York enacted legislation that, in two respects, was to serve as a model for early anti-abortion statutes. First, while barring destruction of an unquickened fetus as well as a quick fetus, it made the former only a misdemeanor, but the latter second-degree manslaughter. Second, it incorporated a concept of therapeutic abortion by providing that an abortion was excused if it "shall have been necessary to preserve the life of such mother, or shall have been advised by two physicians to be necessary for such purpose." By 1840, when Texas had received the common law, only eight American States had statutes dealing with abortion. It was not until after the

War Between the States that legislation began generally to replace the common law. Most of these initial statutes dealt severely with abortion after quickening but were lenient with it before quickening. Most punished attempts equally with completed abortions. While many statutes included the exception for an abortion thought by one or more physicians to be necessary to save the mother's life, that provision soon disappeared and the typical law required that the procedure actually be necessary for that purpose.

Gradually, in the middle and late 19th century the quickening distinction disappeared from the statutory law of most States and the degree of the offense and the penalties were increased. By the end of the 1950's, a large majority of the jurisdictions banned abortion, however and whenever performed, unless done to save or preserve the life of the mother. The exceptions, Alabama and the District of Columbia, permitted abortion to preserve the mother's health. Three States [Massachusetts, New Jersey, and Pennsylvania] permitted abortions that were not "unlawfully" performed or that were not "without lawful justification," leaving interpretation of those standards to the courts. In the past several years, however, a trend toward liberalization of abortion statutes has resulted in adoption, by about one-third of the States, of less stringent laws, most of them patterned after the ALI [American Law Institute]'s Model Penal Code. . . .

It is thus apparent that at common law, at the time of the adoption of our Constitution, and throughout the major portion of the 19th century, abortion was viewed with less disfavor than under most American statutes currently in effect. Phrasing it another way, a woman enjoyed a substantially broader right to terminate a pregnancy than she does in most States today. At least with respect to the early stage of pregnancy, and very possibly without such a limitation, the opportunity to make this choice was present in this country well into the 19th century. Even later, the law continued for some time to treat less punitively an abortion procured in early pregnancy.

6. The position of the American Medical Association. The anti-abortion mood prevalent in this country in the late 19th century was shared by the medical profession. Indeed, the attitude of the profession may have played a significant role in the enactment of stringent criminal abortion legislation during that period.

An AMA Committee on Criminal Abortion was appointed in May 1857. It presented its report to the Twelfth Annual Meeting. That report observed that the Committee had been appointed to investigate criminal abortion "with a view to its general suppression." It deplored abortion and its frequency and it listed three causes of "this general demoralization":

"The first of these causes is a wide-spread popular ignorance of the true character of the crime - a belief, even among mothers themselves, that the foetus is not alive till after the period of quickening.

"The second of the agents alluded to is the fact that the profession themselves are frequently supposed careless of foetal life . . . .

"The third reason of the frightful extent of this crime is found in the grave defects of our laws, both common and statute, as regards the independent and actual existence of the child before birth, as living being. These

errors, which are sufficient in most instances to prevent conviction, are based, and only based, upon mis-
taken and exploded medical dogmas. With strange in-
consistency, the law fully acknowledges the foetus in
utero and its inherent rights, for civil purposes; while
personally and as criminally affected, it fails to recognize it, and to its life as yet denies all protection."

The Committee then offered, and the Association adopted,
resolutions protesting "against such unwarrantable destruction of human life," calling upon state legislatures to
revise their abortion laws, and requesting the cooperation
of state medical societies "in pressing the subject."

In 1871 a long and vivid report was submitted by the
Committee on Criminal Abortion. It ended with the observation, "We had to deal with human life. In a matter
of less importance we could entertain no compromise. An
honest judge on the bench would call things by their
proper names. We could do no less." It proferred resolutions, adopted by the Association, recommending, among
other things, that it "be unlawful and unprofessional for
any physician to induce abortion or premature labor,
without the concurrent opinion of at least one respectable
consulting physician, and then always with a view to the
safety of the child - if that be possible," and calling "the
attention of the clergy of all denominations to the per-
verted views of morality entertained by a large class of
females - aye, and men also, on this important question."

Except for periodic condemnation of the criminal abortionist, no further formal AMA action took place until
1967. In that year, the Committee on Human Reproduc-
tion urged the adoption of a stated policy of opposition to
induced abortion, except when there is "documented medi-

cal evidence" of a threat to the health or life of the mother, or that the child "may be born with incapacitating physical deformity or mental deficiency," or that a pregnancy "resulting from legally established statutory or forcible rape or incest may constitute a threat to the mental or physical health of the patient," and two other physicians "chosen because of their recognized professional competence have examined the patient and have concurred in writing," and the procedure "is performed in a hospital accredited by the Joint Commission on Accreditation of Hospitals." The providing of medical information by physicians to state legislatures in their consideration of legislation regarding therapeutic abortion was "to be considered consistent with the principles of ethics of the American Medical Association." This recommendation was adopted by the House of Delegates.

In 1970, after the introduction of a variety of proposed resolutions, and of a report from its Board of Trustees, a reference committee noted "polarization of the medical profession on this controversial issue"; division among those who had testified; a difference of opinion among AMA councils and committees; "the remarkable shift in testimony" in six months, felt to be influenced "by the rapid changes in state laws and by the judicial decisions which tend to make abortion more freely available";and a feeling "that this trend will continue." On June 25, 1970, the House of Delegates adopted preambles and most of the resolutions proposed by the reference committee. The preambles emphasized "the best interests of the patient," "sound clinical judgment," and "informed patient consent," in contrast to "mere acquiescence to the patient's demand." The resolutions asserted that abortion is a medical procedure that should be performed by a licensed physician in an accredited hospital only after consultation with two other physicians and in conformity with state law, and that no party to the procedure should be required to violate personally held moral principles. The AMA Judicial Council rendered a complementary opinion.

7. The position of the American Public Health Association. In October 1970, the Executive Board of the APHA adopted Standards for Abortion Services. These were five in number:

"a. Rapid and simple abortion referral must be readily available through state and local public health departments, medical societies, or other non-profit organizations.

"b. An important function of counseling should be to simplify and expedite the provision of abortion services; it should not delay the obtaining of these services.

"c. Psychiatric consultation should not be mandatory. As in the case of other specialized medical services, psychiatric consultation should be sought for definite indications and not on a routine basis.

"d. A wide range of individuals from appropriately trained, sympathetic volunteers to highly skilled physicians may qualify as abortion counselors.

"e. Contraception and/or sterilization should be discussed with each abortion patient."

Among factors pertinent to life and health risks associated with abortion were three that "are recognized as important":

"a. the skill of the physician,

"b. the environment in which the abortion is performed, and above all

"c. the duration of pregnancy, as determined by uterine size and confirmed by menstrual history."

It was said that "a well-equipped hospital" offers more protection "to cope with unforeseen difficulties than an office or clinic without such resources. . . . The factor of gestational age is of overriding importance." Thus, it was recommended that abortions in the second trimester and early abortions in the presence of existing medical complications be performed in hospitals as in-patient procedures. For pregnancies in the first trimester, abortion in the hospital with or without overnight stay "is probably the safest practice." An abortion in an extramural facility, however, is an acceptable alternative "provided arrangements exist in advance to admit patients promptly if unforeseen complications develop." Standards for an abortion facility were listed. It was said that at present abortions should be performed by physicians or osteopaths who are licensed to practice and who have "adequate training."

8. The position of the American Bar Association. At its meeting in February 1972 the ABA House of Delegates approved, with 17 opposing votes, the Uniform Abortion Act that had been drafted and approved the preceding August by the Conference of Commissioners on Uniform State Laws. . . .

Three reasons have been advanced to explain historically the enactment of criminal abortion laws in the 19th century and to justify their continued existence.

It has been argued occasionally that these laws were the product of a Victorian social concern to discourage illicit sexual conduct. Texas, however, does not advance this justification in the present case, and it appears that no court or commentator has taken the argument seriously. The appellants and amici [friends of the court] contend, moreover, that this is not a proper state purpose at all and suggest that, if it were, the Texas statutes are overbroad in protecting it since the law fails to distinguish between married and unwed mothers.

A second reason is concerned with abortion as a medical procedure. When most criminal abortion laws were first enacted, the procedure was a hazardous one for the woman. This was particularly true prior to the development of antisepsis. Antiseptic techniques, of course, were based on discoveries by Lister, Pasteur, and others first announced in 1867, but were not generally accepted and employed until about the turn of the century. Abortion mortality was high. Even after 1900, and perhaps until as late as the development of antibiotics in the 1940's, standard modern techniques such as dilation and curettage were not nearly so safe as they are today. Thus, it has been argued that a State's real concern in enacting a criminal abortion law was to protect the pregnant woman, that is, to restrain her from submitting to a procedure that placed her life in serious jeopardy.

Modern medical techniques have altered this situation. [Roe] . . . refer[s] to medical data indicating that abortion in early pregnancy, that is, prior to the end of the first trimester, although not without its risk, is now relatively safe. Mortality rates for women undergoing early abortions, where the procedure is legal, appear to be as low as or lower than the rates for normal childbirth. Consequently, any interest of the State in protecting the woman from an inherently hazardous procedure, except when it would be equally dangerous for her to forgo it, has largely disappeared. Of course, important state interests in the areas of health and medical standards do remain. The State has a legitimate interest in seeing to it that abortion, like any other medical procedure, is performed under circumstances that insure maximum safety for the patient. This interest obviously extends at least to the performing physician and his staff, to the facilities involved, to the availability of after-care, and to adequate provision for any complication or emergency that might arise. The prevalence of high mortality rates at illegal "abortion mills" strengthens, rather than weakens, the State's interest in regulating the conditions under which abortions are performed. Moreover, the risk to the woman increases as her pregnancy continues. Thus, the State retains a definite interest in protecting the woman's own health and safety when an abortion is proposed at a late stage of pregnancy.

The third reason is the State's interest - some phrase it in terms of duty - in protecting prenatal life. Some of the argument for this justification rests on the theory that a new human life is present from the moment of conception. The State's interest and general obligation to protect life then extends, it is argued, to prenatal life. Only when the life of the pregnant mother herself is at stake, balanced against the life she carries within her, should the interest of the embryo or fetus not prevail. Logically, of course, a legitimate state interest in this area need not stand or fall on acceptance of the belief that life begins at conception or at some other point prior to live birth. In assessing the State's interest, recognition may be given to the less rigid claim that as long as at least *potential* life is involved, the State may assert interests beyond the protection of the pregnant woman alone.

Parties challenging state abortion laws have sharply disputed in some courts the contention that a purpose of these laws, when enacted, was to protect prenatal life. Pointing to the absence of legislative history to support the contention, they claim that most state laws were designed solely to protect the woman. Because medical advances have lessened this concern, at least with respect to abortion in early pregnancy, they argue that with respect to such abortions the laws can no longer be justified by any state interest. There is some scholarly support for this view of original purpose. The few state courts called upon to interpret their laws in the late 19th and early 20th centuries did focus on the State's interest in protecting the woman's health rather than in preserving the embryo and fetus. Proponents of this view point out that in many States, including Texas, by statute or judicial interpretation, the pregnant woman herself could not be prosecuted for self-abortion or for cooperating in an abortion performed upon her by another. They claim that adoption of the "quickening" distinction through received common law and state statutes tacitly recognizes the greater health hazards inherent in late abortion and impliedly repudiates the theory that life begins at conception.

It is with these interests, and the weight to be attached to them, that this case is concerned.

The Constitution does not explicitly mention any right of privacy. In a line of decisions, however, going back perhaps as far as *Union Pacific R. Co. v. Botsford*, the Court has recognized that a right of personal privacy, or a guarantee of certain areas or zones of privacy, does exist under the Constitution. In varying contexts, the Court or individual Justices have, indeed, found at least the roots of that right in the First Amendment; in the Fourth and Fifth Amendments; in the penumbras of the Bill of Rights; in the Ninth Amendment; or in the concept of liberty guaranteed by the first section of the Fourteenth Amendment. . . . [O]nly personal rights that can be deemed "fundamental" or "implicit in the concept of ordered liberty" are included in this guarantee of personal privacy. . . . [T]he right has some extension to activities relating to marriage; procreation; contraception; family relationships; and child rearing and education.

This right of privacy, whether it be founded in the Fourteenth Amendment's concept of personal liberty and restrictions upon state action, as we feel it is, or, as the District Court determined, in the Ninth Amendment's reservation of rights to the people, is broad enough to encompass a woman's decision whether or not to terminate her pregnancy. The detriment that the State would impose upon the pregnant woman by denying this choice altogether is apparent. Specific and direct harm medically diagnosable even in early pregnancy may be involved. Maternity, or additional offspring, may force upon the woman a distressful life and future. Psychological harm may be imminent. Mental and physical health may be taxed by child care. There is also the distress, for all concerned, associated with the unwanted child, and there is the problem of bringing a child into a family already unable, psychologically and otherwise, to care for it. In other cases, as in this one, the additional difficulties and continuing stigma of unwed motherhood may be involved. All these are factors the woman and her responsible physician necessarily will consider in consultation.

On the basis of elements such as these, [Roe] argue[s] that the woman's right is absolute and that she is entitled to terminate her pregnancy at whatever time, in whatever way, and for whatever reason she alone chooses. With this we do not agree. [Roe]'s arguments that Texas either has no valid interest at all in regulating the abortion decision, or no interest strong enough to support any limitation upon the woman's sole determination, are unpersuasive. The Court's decisions recognizing a right of privacy also acknowledge that some state regulation in areas protected by that right is appropriate. As noted above, a State may properly assert important interests in safeguarding health, in maintaining medical standards, and in protecting potential life. At some point in pregnancy, these respective interests become sufficiently compelling to sustain regulation of the factors that govern the abortion decision. The privacy right involved, therefore, cannot be said to be absolute. In fact, it is not clear to us that the claim . . . that one has an unlimited right to do with one's body as one pleases bears a close relationship to the right of privacy previously articulated in the Court's decisions. The Court has refused to recognize an unlimited right of this kind in the past.

We, therefore, conclude that the right of personal privacy includes the abortion decision, but that this right is not unqualified and must be considered against important state interests in regulation.

We note that those federal and state courts that have recently considered abortion law challenges have reached the same conclusion. A majority, in addition to the District Court in the present case, have held state laws unconstitutional, at least in part, because of vagueness or because of overbreadth and abridgment of rights.

Others have sustained state statutes.

Although the results are divided, most of these courts have agreed that the right of privacy, however based, is broad enough to cover the abortion decision; that the right, nonetheless, is not absolute and is subject to some limitations; and that at some point the state interests as to protection of health, medical standards, and prenatal life, become dominant. We agree with this approach.

Where certain "fundamental rights" are involved, the Court has held that regulation limiting these rights may be justified only by a "compelling state interest," and that legislative enactments must be narrowly drawn to express only the legitimate state interests at stake.

In the recent abortion cases . . . courts have recognized these principles. Those striking down state laws have generally scrutinized the State's interests in protecting health and potential life, and have concluded that neither interest justified broad limitations on the reasons for which a physician and his pregnant patient might decide that she should have an abortion in the early stages of pregnancy. Courts sustaining [letting stand] state laws have held that the State's determinations to protect health or prenatal life are dominant and constitutionally justifiable.

The District Court held that [Wade] failed to meet his burden of demonstrating that the Texas statute's infringement upon Roe's rights was necessary to support a compelling state interest, and that, although [Wade] presented "several compelling justifications for state presence in the area of abortions," the statutes outstripped these justifications and swept "far beyond any areas of compelling state interest." [Roe] and [Wade] both contest that holding.

[Roe], as has been indicated, claims an absolute right that bars any state imposition of criminal penalties in the area. [Wade] argues that the State's determination to recognize and protect prenatal life from and after conception constitutes a compelling state interest. As noted above, we do not agree fully with either formulation.

A. [Wade] and certain amici argue that the fetus is a "person" within the language and meaning of the Fourteenth Amendment. In support of this, they outline at length and in detail the well-known facts of fetal development. If this suggestion of personhood is established, [Roe]'s case, of course, collapses, for the fetus' right to life is then guaranteed specifically by the Amendment. [Roe] conceded as much on reargument. On the other hand, [Wade] conceded on reargument that no case could be cited that holds that a fetus is a person within the meaning of the Fourteenth Amendment.

The Constitution does not define "person" in so many words. Section 1 of the Fourteenth Amendment contains three references to "person." The first, in defining "citizens," speaks of "persons born or naturalized in the United States." The word also appears both in the Due Process Clause and in the Equal Protection Clause. "Person" is used in other places in the Constitution: in the listing of qualifications for Representatives and Senators; in the Apportionment Clause; in the Migration and Importation provision; in the Emolument Clause; in the Electors provisions; in the provision outlining qualifications for the office of President; in the Extradition provisions; and in the Fifth, Twelfth, and Twenty-second Amendments, as well as in [Sections] 2 and 3 of the Fourteenth Amendment. But in nearly all these instances, the use of the word is such that it has application only postnatally. None indicates, with any assurance, that it has any possible pre-natal application.

All this, together with our observation that throughout the major portion of the 19th century prevailing legal abortion practices were far freer than they are today, persuades us that the word "person," as used in the Fourteenth Amendment, does not include the unborn. This is in accord with the results reached in those few cases where the issue has been squarely presented. Indeed, our decision in *United States v. Vuitch* inferentially is to the same effect, for we there would not have indulged in statutory interpretation favorable to abortion in specified circumstances if the necessary consequence was the termination of life entitled to Fourteenth Amendment protection.

This conclusion, however, does not of itself fully answer the contentions raised by Texas, and we pass on to other considerations.

B. The pregnant woman cannot be isolated in her privacy. She carries an embryo and, later, a fetus, if one accepts the medical definitions of the developing young in the human uterus. The situation therefore is inherently different from marital intimacy, or bedroom possession of obscene material, or marriage, or procreation, or education. ... As we have intimated above, it is reasonable and appropriate for a State to decide that at some point in time another interest, that of health of the mother or that of potential human life, becomes significantly involved. The woman's privacy is no longer sole and any right of privacy she possesses must be measured accordingly.

Texas urges that, apart from the Fourteenth Amendment, life begins at conception and is present throughout pregnancy, and that, therefore, the State has a compelling interest in protecting that life from and after conception. We need not resolve the difficult question of when life begins. When those trained in the respective disciplines of medicine, philosophy, and theology are unable to arrive at any consensus, the judiciary, at this point in the development of man's knowledge, is not in a position to speculate as to the answer.

It should be sufficient to note briefly the wide divergence of thinking on this most sensitive and difficult question. There has always been strong support for the view that life does not begin until live birth. This was the belief of the Stoics. It appears to be the predominant, though not the unanimous, attitude of the Jewish faith. It may be taken to represent also the position of a large segment of the Protestant community, insofar as that can be ascertained; organized groups that have taken a formal position on the abortion issue have generally regarded abortion as a matter for the conscience of the individual and her family. As we have noted, the common law found greater significance in quickening. Physicians and their scientific colleagues have regarded that event with less interest and have tended to focus either upon conception, upon live birth, or upon the interim point at which the fetus becomes "viable," that is, potentially able to live outside the mother's womb, albeit with artificial aid. Viability is usually placed at about seven months (28 weeks) but may occur earlier, even at 24 weeks. The Aristotelian theory of "mediate animation," that held sway throughout the Middle Ages and the Renaissance in Europe, continued to be official Roman Catholic dogma until the 19th century, despite opposition to this "ensoulment" theory from those in the Church who would recognize the existence of life from the moment of conception. The latter is now, of course, the official belief of the Catholic Church. As one of the briefs amicus discloses, this is a view strongly held by many non-Catholics as well, and by many physicians. Substantial problems for precise definition of this view are posed, however, by new embryological data that purport to indicate that conception is a "process" over time, rather than an event, and by new medical techniques such as menstrual extraction, the "morning-after" pill, implantation of embryos, artificial insemination, and even artificial wombs.

In areas other than criminal abortion, the law has been reluctant to endorse any theory that life, as we recognize it, begins before live birth or to accord legal rights to the unborn except in narrowly defined situations and except when the rights are contingent upon live birth. For example, the traditional rule of tort law denied recovery for prenatal injuries even though the child was born alive. That rule has been changed in almost every jurisdiction. In most States, recovery is said to be permitted only if the fetus was viable, or at least quick, when the injuries were sustained, though few courts have squarely so held. In a recent development, generally opposed by the commentators, some States permit the parents of a stillborn child to maintain an action for wrongful death because of prenatal injuries. Such an action, however, would appear to be one to vindicate the parents' interest and is thus consistent with the view that the fetus, at most, represents only the potentiality of life. Similarly, unborn children have been recognized as acquiring rights or interests by way of inheritance or other devolution of property, and have been represented by [legal representatives]. Perfection of the interests involved, again, has generally been contingent upon live birth. In short, the unborn have never been recognized in the law as persons in the whole sense.

In view of all this, we do not agree that, by adopting one theory of life, Texas may override the rights of the pregnant woman that are at stake. We repeat, however, that the State does have an important and legitimate interest in preserving and protecting the health of the pregnant woman, whether she be a resident of the State or a nonresident who seeks medical consultation and treatment there, and that it has still *another* important and legitimate interest in protecting the potentiality of human life. These interests are separate and distinct. Each grows in substantiality as the woman approaches term and, at a point during pregnancy, each becomes "compelling."

With respect to the State's important and legitimate interest in the health of the mother, the "compelling" point, in the light of present medical knowledge, is at approximately the end of the first trimester. This is so because of the now-established medical fact that until the end of the first trimester mortality in abortion may be less than mortality in normal childbirth. It follows that, from and after this point, a State may regulate the abortion procedure to the extent that the regulation reasonably relates to the preservation and protection of maternal health. Examples of permissible state regulation in this area are requirements as to the qualifications of the person who is to perform the abortion; as to the licensure of that person; as to the facility in which the procedure is to be performed, that is, whether it must be a hospital or may be a clinic or some other place of less-than-hospital status; as to the licensing of the facility; and the like.

This means, on the other hand, that, for the period of pregnancy prior to this "compelling" point, the attending physician, in consultation with his patient, is free to determine, without regulation by the State, that, in his medical judgment, the patient's pregnancy should be terminated. If that decision is reached, the judgment may be effectuated by an abortion free of interference by the State.

With respect to the State's important and legitimate interest in potential life, the "compelling" point is at viability. This is so because the fetus then presumably has the capability of meaningful life outside the mother's womb. State regulation protective of fetal life after viability thus has both logical and biological justifications. If the State is interested in protecting fetal life after viability, it may go so far as to proscribe [prohibit] abortion during that period, except when it is necessary to preserve the life or health of the mother.

Measured against these standards, [Article] 1196 of the Texas Penal Code, in restricting legal abortions to those "procured or attempted by medical advice for the purpose of saving the life of the mother," sweeps too broadly. The statute makes no distinction between abortions performed early in pregnancy and those performed later, and it limits to a single reason, "saving" the mother's life, the legal justification for the procedure. The statute, therefore, cannot survive the constitutional attack made upon it here. . .

To summarize and to repeat:

1. A state criminal abortion statute of the current Texas type, that excepts from criminality only a *lifesaving* procedure on behalf of the mother, without regard to pregnancy stage and without recognition of the other interests involved, is violative of the Due Process Clause of the Fourteenth Amendment.

(a) For the stage prior to approximately the end of the first trimester, the abortion decision and its effectuation must be left to the medical judgment of the pregnant woman's attending physician.

(b) For the stage subsequent to approximately the end of the first trimester, the State, in promoting its interest in the health of the mother, may, if it chooses, regulate the abortion procedure in ways that are reasonably related to maternal health.

(c) For the stage subsequent to viability, the State in promoting its interest in the potentiality of human life may, if it chooses, regulate, and even proscribe, abortion except where it is necessary, in appropriate medical judgment, for the preservation of the life or health of the mother.

2. The State may define the term "physician" . . . to mean only a physician currently licensed by the State, and may proscribe any abortion by a person who is not a physician as so defined. . . .

This holding, we feel, is consistent with the relative weights of the respective interests involved, with the lessons and examples of medical and legal history, with the lenity of the common law, and with the demands of the profound problems of the present day. The decision leaves the State free to place increasing restrictions on abortion as the period of pregnancy lengthens, so long as those restrictions are tailored to the recognized state interests. The decision vindicates the right of the physician to administer medical treatment according to his professional judgment up to the points where important state interests provide compelling justifications for intervention. Up to those points, the abortion decision in all its aspects is inherently, and primarily, a medical decision, and basic responsibility for it must rest with the physician. If an individual practitioner abuses the privilege of exercising proper medical judgment, the usual remedies, judicial and intra-professional, are available.

Our conclusion that [Article] 1196 is unconstitutional means, of course, that the Texas abortion statutes, as a unit, must fall. . . .

CHIEF JUSTICE BURGER, concurring: I agree that, under the Fourteenth Amendment to the Constitution, the abortion statutes of Georgia and Texas impermissibly limit the performance of abortions necessary to protect the health of pregnant women, using the term health in its broadest medical context. I am somewhat troubled that the Court has taken notice of various scientific and medical data in reaching its conclusion; however, I do not believe that the Court has exceeded the scope of judicial notice accepted in other contexts.

In oral argument, counsel for the State of Texas informed the Court that early abortive procedures were routinely permitted in certain exceptional cases, such as noncensual pregnancies resulting from rape and incest. In the face of a rigid and narrow statute, such as that of Texas, no one in these circumstances should be placed in a posture of dependence on a prosecutorial policy or prosecutorial discretion. Of course, States must have broad power, within the limits indicated in the opinions, to regulate the subject of abortions, but where the consequences of state intervention are so severe, uncertainty must be avoided as much as possible. For my part, I would be inclined to allow a State to require the certification of two physicians to support an abortion, but the Court holds otherwise. I do not believe that such a procedure is unduly burdensome, as are the complex steps of the Georgia statute [in *Doe v. Bolton*], which require as many as six doctors and the use of a hospital certified by the JCAH.

I do not read the Court's holdings today as having the sweeping consequences attributed to them by the dissenting Justices; the dissenting views discount the reality that the vast majority of physicians observe the standards of their profession, and act only on the basis of carefully deliberated medical judgments relating to life and health. Plainly, the Court today rejects any claim that the Constitution requires abortion on demand.

JUSTICE DOUGLAS, concurring [This opinion also applies to *Doe v. Bolton*]: While I join the opinion of the Court, I add a few words.

The questions presented in the present cases go far beyond the issues of vagueness, which we considered in *United States v. Vuitch*. They involve the right of privacy, one aspect of which we considered in *Griswold v. Connecticut*, when we held that various guarantees in the Bill of Rights create zones of privacy.

The *Griswold* case involved a law forbidding the use of contraceptives. We held that law as applied to married people unconstitutional:

"We deal with a right of privacy older than the Bill of Rights - older than our political parties, older than our school system. Marriage is a coming together for better or for worse, hopefully enduring, and intimate to the degree of being sacred."

The District Court in *Doe* held that *Griswold* and related
cases "establish a Constitutional right to privacy broad
enough to encompass the right of a woman to terminate
an unwanted pregnancy in its early stages, by obtaining an
abortion."

The Supreme Court of California expressed the same view
in *People v. Belous*.

The Ninth Amendment obviously does not create federally enforceable rights. It merely says, "The enumeration in
the Constitution, of certain rights, shall not be construed
to deny or disparage others retained by the people." But a
catalogue of these rights includes customary, traditional,
and time-honored rights, amenities, privileges, and immunities that come within the sweep of "the Blessings of Liberty" mentioned in the preamble to the Constitution.
Many of them, in my view, come within the meaning of
the term "liberty" as used in the Fourteenth Amendment.

*First is the autonomous control over the development and
expression of one's intellect, interests, tastes, and personality.*

These are rights protected by the First Amendment and,
in my view, they are absolute, permitting of no exceptions. The Free Exercise Clause of the First Amendment
is one facet of this constitutional right. The right to remain silent as respects one's own beliefs is protected by
the First and the Fifth. The First Amendment grants the
privacy of first-class mail. All of these aspects of the
right of privacy are rights "retained by the people" in the
meaning of the Ninth Amendment.

Second is freedom of choice in the basic decisions of one's life respecting marriage, divorce, procreation, contraception, and the education and upbringing of children.

These rights, unlike those protected by the First Amendment, are subject to some control by the police power. Thus, the Fourth Amendment speaks only of "unreasonable searches and seizures" and of "probable cause." These rights are "fundamental," and we have held that in order to support legislative action the statute must be narrowly and precisely drawn and that a "compelling state interest" must be shown in support of the limitation.

The liberty to marry a person of one's own choosing; the right of procreation; the liberty to direct the education of one's children; and the privacy of the marital relation are in this category. Only last Term in *Eisenstadt v. Baird*, another contraceptive case, we expanded the concept of *Griswold* by saying:

"It is true that in *Griswold* the right of privacy in question inhered in the marital relationship. Yet the marital couple is not an independent entity with a mind and heart of its own, but an association of two individuals each with a separate intellectual and emotional makeup. If the right of privacy means anything, it is the right of the *individual*, married or single, to be free from unwarranted governmental intrusion into matters so fundamentally affecting a person as the decision whether to bear or beget a child."

This right of privacy was called by Justice Brandeis the right "to be let alone." That right includes the privilege of an individual to plan his own affairs, for, "'outside areas of plainly harmful conduct, every American is left to shape his own life as he thinks best, do what he pleases, go where he pleases.'"

Third is the freedom to care for one's health and person, freedom from bodily restraint or compulsion, freedom to walk, stroll, or loaf.

These rights, though fundamental, are likewise subject to regulation on a showing of "compelling state interest." We stated in *Papachristou v. City of Jacksonville* that walking, strolling, and wandering "are historically part of the amenities of life as we have know them." As stated in *Jacobson v. Massachusetts:*

"There is, of course, a sphere within which the individual may assert the supremacy of his own will and rightfully dispute the authority of any human government, especially of any free government existing under a written constitution, to interfere with the exercise of that will."

. . . . In *Terry v. Ohio*, the Court, in speaking of the Fourth Amendment, stated, "This inestimable right of personal security belongs as much to the citizen on the streets of our cities as to the homeowner closeted in his study to dispose of his secret affairs."

. . . . In *Meyer v. Nebraska*, the Court said:

"Without doubt, it [liberty] denotes not merely freedom from bodily restraint but also the right of the individual to contract, to engage in any of the common occupations of life, to acquire useful knowledge, to marry, establish a home and bring up children, to worship God according to the dictates of his own conscience, and generally to enjoy those privileges long recognized at common law as essential to the orderly pursuit of happiness by free men."

The Georgia statute is at war with the clear message of these cases - that a woman is free to make the basic decision whether to bear an unwanted child. Elaborate argument is hardly necessary to demonstrate that childbirth may deprive a woman of her preferred lifestyle and force upon her a radically different and undesired future. For example, rejected applicants under the Georgia statute are required to endure the discomforts of pregnancy; to incur the pain, higher mortality rate, and aftereffects of childbirth; to abandon educational plans; to sustain loss of income; to forgo the satisfactions of careers; to tax further mental and physical health in providing child care; and, in some cases, to bear the lifelong stigma of unwed motherhood, a badge which may haunt, if not deter, later legitimate family relationships.

Such reasoning is, however, only the beginning of the problem. The State has interests to protect. Vaccinations to prevent epidemics are one example, as *Jacobson* holds. The Court held that compulsory sterilization of imbeciles afflicted with hereditary forms of insanity or imbecility is another. Abortion affects another. While childbirth endangers the lives of some women, voluntary abortion at any time and place regardless of medical standards would impinge on a rightful concern of society. The woman's health is part of that concern; as is the life of the fetus after quickening. These concerns justify the State in treating the procedure as a medical one.

One difficulty is that this statute as construed and applied apparently does not give full sweep to the "psychological as well as physical well-being" of women patients which saved the concept "health" from being void for vagueness in *United States v. Vuitch*. But, apart from that, Georgia's enactment has a constitutional infirmity because . . . it "limits the number of reasons for which an abortion may be sought." I agree with the holding of the District Court, "This the State may not do, because such action unduly restricts a decision sheltered by the Constitutional right to privacy."

The vicissitudes of life produce pregnancies which may be unwanted, or which may impair "health" in the broad *Vuitch* sense of the term, or which may imperil the life of the mother, or which in the full setting of the case may create such suffering, dislocations, misery, or tragedy as to make an early abortion the only civilized step to take. These hardships may be properly embraced in the "health" factor of the mother as appraised by a person of insight. Or they may be part of a broader medical judgment based on what is "appropriate" in a given case, though perhaps not "necessary" in a strict sense.

The "liberty" of the mother, though rooted as it is in the Constitution, may be qualified by the State for the reasons we have stated. But where fundamental personal rights and liberties are involved, the corrective legislation must be "narrowly drawn to prevent the supposed evil," and not be dealt with in an "unlimited and indiscriminate" manner. Unless regulatory measures are so confined and are addressed to the specific areas of compelling legislative concern, the police power would become the great leveler of constitutional rights and liberties.

There is no doubt that the State may require abortions to be performed by qualified medical personnel. The legitimate objective of preserving the mother's health clearly supports such laws. Their impact upon the woman's privacy is minimal. But the Georgia statute outlaws virtually all such operations - even in the earliest stages of pregnancy. In light of modern medical evidence suggesting that an early abortion is safer healthwise than childbirth itself, it cannot be seriously urged that so comprehensive a ban is aimed at protecting the woman's health. Rather, this expansive proscription of all abortions along the temporal spectrum can rest only on a public goal of preserving both embryonic and fetal life.

The present statute has struck the balance between the woman's and the State's interests wholly in favor of the latter. I am not prepared to hold that a State may equate, as Georgia has done, all phases of maturation preceding birth. We held in *Griswold* that the States may not preclude spouses from attempting to avoid the joinder of sperm and egg. If this is true, it is difficult to perceive any overriding public necessity which might attach precisely at the moment of conception. As Justice Clark has said:

"To say that life is present at conception is to give recognition to the potential, rather than the actual. The unfertilized egg has life, and if fertilized, it takes on human proportions. But the law deals in reality, not obscurity - the known rather than the unknown. When sperm meets egg life may eventually form, but quite often it does not. The law does not deal in speculation. The phenomenon of life takes time to develop, and until it is actually present, it cannot be destroyed. Its interruption prior to formation would hardly be homicide, and as we have seen, society does not regard it as such. The rites of Baptism are not performed and death certificates are not required when a miscarriage occurs. No prosecutor has ever returned a murder indictment charging the taking of the life of a fetus. This would not be the case if the fetus constituted human life."

In summary, the enactment is overbroad. It is not closely correlated to the aim of preserving prenatal life. In fact, it permits its destruction in several cases, including pregnancies resulting from sex acts in which unmarried females are below the statutory age of consent. At the same time, however, the measure broadly proscribes aborting other pregnancies which may cause severe mental disorders. Additionally, the statute is overbroad because it equates the value of embryonic life immediately after conception with the worth of life immediately before birth.

Under the Georgia Act, the mother's physician is not the sole judge as to whether the abortion should be performed. Two other licensed physicians must concur in his judgment. Moreover, the abortion must be performed in a licensed hospital; and the abortion must be approved in advance by a committee of the medical staff of that hospital.

Physicians . . . complain of the Georgia Act's interference with their practice of their profession.

The right of privacy has no more conspicuous place than in the physician-patient relationship, unless it be in the priest-penitent relation.

It is one thing for a patient to agree that her physician may consult with another physician about her case. It is quite a different matter for the State compulsorily to impose on that physician-patient relationship another layer or, as in this case, still a third layer of physicians. The right of privacy - the right to care for one's health and person and to seek out a physician of one's own choice protected by the Fourteenth Amendment - becomes only a matter of theory, not a reality, when a multiple-physician-approval system is mandated by the State.

The State licenses a physician. If he is derelict or faithless, the procedures available to punish him or to deprive him of his license are well known. He is entitled to procedural due process before professional disciplinary sanctions may be imposed. Crucial here, however, is state-imposed control over the medical decision whether pregnancy should be interrupted. The good-faith decision of the patient's chosen physician is overridden and the final decision passed on to others in whose selection the patient has no part. This is a total destruction of the right of privacy between physician and patient and the intimacy of relation which that entails.

The right to seek advice on one's health and the right to place reliance on the physician of one's choice are basic to Fourteenth Amendment values. We deal with fundamental rights and liberties, which, as already noted, can be contained or controlled only by discretely drawn legislation that preserves the "liberty" and regulates only those phases of the problem of compelling legislative concern. The imposition by the State of group controls over the physician-patient relationship is not made on any medical procedure apart from abortion, no matter how dangerous the medical step may be. The oversight imposed on the physician and patient in abortion cases denies them their "liberty," [that is,] their right of privacy, without any compelling, discernible state interest.

Georgia has constitutional warrant in treating abortion as a medical problem. To protect the woman's right of privacy, however, the control must be through the physician of her choice and the standards set for his performance.

The protection of the fetus when it has acquired life is a legitimate concern of the State. Georgia's law makes no rational, discernible decision on that score. For under the Code, the developmental stage of the fetus is irrelevant when pregnancy is the result of rape, when the fetus will very likely be born with a permanent defect, or when a continuation of the pregnancy will endanger the life of the mother or permanently injure her health. When life is present is a question we do not try to resolve. While basically a question for medical experts, . . . it is, of course, caught up in matters of religion and morality.

In short, I agree with the Court that endangering the life of the woman or seriously and permanently injuring her health are standards too narrow for the right of privacy that is at stake.

I also agree that the superstructure of medical supervision which Georgia has erected violates the patient's right of privacy inherent in her choice of her own physician.

JUSTICE STEWART, concurring: In 1963, this Court, in *Ferguson v. Skrupa*, purported to sound the death knell for the doctrine of substantive due process, a doctrine under which many state laws had in the past been held to violate the Fourteenth Amendment. As Justice Black's opinion for the Court in *Skrupa* put it: "We have returned to the original constitutional proposition that courts do not substitute their social and economic beliefs for the judgment of legislative bodies, who are elected to pass laws."

Barely two years later, in *Griswold v. Connecticut*, the Court held a Connecticut birth control law unconstitutional. . . . [I]t was clear to me then, and it is equally clear to me now, that the *Griswold* decision can be rationally understood only as a holding that the Connecticut statute substantively invaded the "liberty" that is protected by the Due Process Clause of the Fourteenth Amendment. As so understood, *Griswold* stands as one in a long line of pre-*Skrupa* cases decided under the doctrine of substantive due process, and I now accept it as such.

"In a Constitution for a free people, there can be no doubt that the meaning of 'liberty' must be broad indeed." The Constitution nowhere mentions a specific right of personal choice in matters of marriage and family life, but the "liberty" protected by the Due Process Clause of the Fourteenth Amendment covers more than those freedoms explicitly named in the Bill of Rights.

As Justice Harlan once wrote: "[T]he full scope of the liberty guaranteed by the Due Process Clause cannot be found in or limited by the precise terms of the specific guarantees elsewhere provided in the Constitution. This 'liberty' is not a series of isolated points pricked out in terms of the taking of property; the freedom of speech, press, and religion; the right to keep and bear arms; the freedom from unreasonable searches and seizures; and so on. It is a rational continuum which, broadly speaking, includes a freedom from all substantial arbitrary impositions and purposeless restraints . . . and which also recognizes, what a reasonable and sensitive judgment must, that certain interests require particularly careful scrutiny of the state needs asserted to justify their abridgment." In the words of Justice Frankfurter, "Great concepts like . . . 'liberty' . . . were purposely left to gather meaning from experience. For they relate to the whole domain of social and economic fact, and the statesmen who founded this Nation knew too well that only a stagnant society remains unchanged."

Several decisions of this Court make clear that freedom of personal choice in matters of marriage and family life is one of the liberties protected by the Due Process Clause of the Fourteenth Amendment. As recently as last Term, in *Eisenstadt v. Baird*, we recognized "the right of the *individual*, married or single, to be free from unwarranted governmental intrusion into matters so fundamentally affecting a person as the decision whether to bear or beget a child." That right necessarily includes the right of a woman to decide whether or not to terminate her pregnancy. "Certainly the interests of a woman in giving of her physical and emotional self during pregnancy and the interests that will be affected throughout her life by the birth and raising of a child are of a far greater degree of significance and personal intimacy than the right to send a child to private school protected in *Pierce v. Society of Sisters*, or the right to teach a foreign language protected in *Meyer v. Nebraska*.

Clearly, therefore, the Court today is correct in holding that the right asserted by Jane Roe is embraced within the personal liberty protected by the Due Process Clause of the Fourteenth Amendment.

It is evident that the Texas abortion statute infringes that right directly. Indeed, it is difficult to imagine a more complete abridgment of a constitutional freedom than that worked by the inflexible criminal statute now in force in Texas. The question then becomes whether the state interests advanced to justify this abridgment can survive the "particularly careful scrutiny" that the Fourteenth Amendment here requires.

The asserted state interests are protection of the health and safety of the pregnant woman, and protection of the potential future human life within her. These are legitimate objectives, amply sufficient to permit a State to regulate abortions as it does other surgical procedures, and perhaps sufficient to permit a State to regulate abortions more stringently or even to prohibit them in the late stages of pregnancy. But such legislation is not before us, and I think the Court today has thoroughly demonstrated that these state interests cannot constitutionally support the broad abridgment of personal liberty worked by the existing Texas law. Accordingly, I join the Court's opinion holding that that law is invalid under the Due Process Clause of the Fourteenth Amendment.

JUSTICE WHITE (joined by Justice Rehnquist), dissenting [This opinion also applies to *Doe v. Bolton*]: At the heart of the controversy in these cases are those recurring pregnancies that pose no danger whatsoever to the life or health of the mother but are, nevertheless, unwanted for any one or more of a variety of reasons - convenience, family planning, economics, dislike of children, the embarrassment of illegitimacy, etc. The common claim before us is that for any one of such reasons, or for no reason at all, and without asserting or claiming any threat to life or health, any woman is entitled to an abortion at her request if she is able to find a medical advisor willing to undertake the procedure.

The Court for the most part sustains this position: During the period prior to the time the fetus becomes viable, the Constitution of the United States values the convenience, whim, or caprice of the putative mother more than the life or potential life of the fetus; the Constitution, therefore, guarantees the right to an abortion as against any state law or policy seeking to protect the fetus from an abortion not prompted by more compelling reasons of the mother.

With all due respect, I dissent. I find nothing in the language or history of the Constitution to support the Court's judgment. The Court simply fashions and announces a new constitutional right for pregnant mothers and, with scarcely any reason or authority for its action, invests that right with sufficient substance to override most existing state abortion statutes. The upshot is that the people and the legislatures of the 50 States are constitutionally disentitled to weigh the relative importance of the continued existence and development of the fetus, on the one hand, against a spectrum of possible impacts on the mother, on the other hand. As an exercise of raw judicial power, the Court perhaps has authority to do what it does today; but in my view its judgment is an improvident and extravagant exercise of the power of judicial review that the Constitution extends to this Court.

The Court apparently values the convenience of the pregnant mother more than the continued existence and development of the life or potential life that she carries. Whether or not I might agree with that marshaling of values, I can in no event join the Court's judgment because I find no constitutional warrant for imposing such an order of priorities on the people and legislatures of the States. In a sensitive area such as this, involving as it does issues over which reasonable men may easily and heatedly differ, I cannot accept the Court's exercise of its clear power of choice by interposing a constitutional barrier to state efforts to protect human life and by investing mothers and doctors with the constitutionally protected right to exterminate it. This issue, for the most part, should be left with the people and to the political processes the people have devised to govern their affairs.

It is my view, therefore, that the Texas statute is not constitutionally infirm because it denies abortions to those who seek to serve only their convenience rather than to protect their life or health. Nor is this plaintiff, who claims no threat to her mental or physical health, entitled to assert the possible rights of those women whose pregnancy assertedly implicates their health. . . .

I would reverse the judgment of the District Court in the Georgia case.

JUSTICE WILLIAM REHNQUIST, dissenting: The Court's opinion brings to the decision of this troubling question both extensive historical fact and a wealth of legal scholarship. While the opinion thus commands my respect, I find myself nonetheless in fundamental disagreement with those parts of it that invalidate the Texas statute in question, and therefore dissent.

The Court's opinion decides that a State may impose virtually no restriction on the performance of abortions during the first trimester of pregnancy. Our previous decisions indicate that a necessary predicate for such an opinion is a plaintiff who was in her first trimester of pregnancy at some time during the pendency of her lawsuit. While a party may vindicate his own constitutional rights, he may not seek vindication for the rights of others. The Court's statement of facts in this case makes clear, however, that the record in no way indicates the presence of such a plaintiff. We know only that plaintiff Roe at the time of filing her complaint was a pregnant woman; for aught that appears in this record, she may have been in her *last* trimester of pregnancy as of the date the complaint was filed.

Nothing in the Court's opinion indicates that Texas might not constitutionally apply its proscription of abortion as written to a woman in that stage of pregnancy. Nonetheless, the Court uses her complaint against the Texas statute as a fulcrum for deciding that States may impose virtually no restrictions on medical abortions performed during the *first* trimester of pregnancy. In deciding such a hypothetical lawsuit, the Court departs from the longstanding admonition that it should never "formulate a rule of constitutional law broader than is required by the precise facts to which it is to be applied."

Even if there were a plaintiff in this case capable of litigating the issue which the Court decides, I would reach a conclusion opposite to that reached by the Court. I have difficulty in concluding, as the Court does, that the right of "privacy" is involved in this case. Texas, by the statute here challenged, bars the performance of a medical abortion by a licensed physician on a plaintiff such as Roe. A transaction resulting in an operation such as this is not "private" in the ordinary usage of that word. Nor is the "privacy" that the Court finds here even a distant relative of the freedom from searches and seizures protected by the Fourth Amendment to the Constitution, which the Court has referred to as embodying a right to privacy.

If the Court means by the term "privacy" no more than that the claim of a person to be free from unwanted state regulation of consensual transactions may be a form of "liberty" protected by the Fourteenth Amendment, there is no doubt that similar claims have been upheld in our earlier decisions on the basis of that liberty. I agree with the statement of Justice Stewart in his concurring opinion that the "liberty," against deprivation of which without due process the Fourteenth Amendment protects, embraces more than the rights found in the Bill of Rights. But that liberty is not guaranteed absolutely against deprivation, only against deprivation without due process of law. The test traditionally applied in the area of social and economic legislation is whether or not a law such as that challenged has a rational relation to a valid state objective. The Due Process Clause of the Fourteenth Amendment undoubtedly does place a limit, albeit a broad one, on legislative power to enact laws such as this. If the Texas statute were to prohibit an abortion even where the mother's life is in jeopardy, I have little doubt that such a statute would lack a rational relation to a valid state objective under the test stated in *Williamson*. But the Court's sweeping invalidation of any restrictions on abortion during the first trimester is impossible to justify under that standard, and the conscious weighing of competing factors that the Court's opinion apparently substitutes for the established test is far more appropriate to a legislative judgment than to a judicial one.

The Court eschews the history of the Fourteenth Amendment in its reliance on the "compelling state interest" test. But the Court adds a new wrinkle to this test by transposing it from the legal considerations associated with the Equal Protection Clause of the Fourteenth Amendment to this case arising under the Due Process Clause of the Fourteenth Amendment. Unless I misapprehend the consequences of this transplanting of the "compelling state interest test," the Court's opinion will accomplish the seemingly impossible feat of leaving this area of the law more confused than it found it.

. . . . As in *Lochner* [*v. New York*] and similar cases applying substantive due process standards to economic and social welfare legislation, the adoption of the compelling state interest standard will inevitably require this Court to examine the legislative policies and pass on the wisdom of these policies in the very process of deciding whether a particular state interest put forward may or may not be "compelling." The decision here to break pregnancy into three distinct terms and to outline the permissible restrictions the State may impose in each one, for example, partakes more of judicial legislation than it does of a determination of the intent of the drafters of the Fourteenth Amendment.

The fact that a majority of the States reflecting, after all, the majority sentiment in those States, have had restrictions on abortions for at least a century is a strong indication, it seems to me, that the asserted right to an abortion is not "so rooted in the traditions and conscience of our people as to be ranked as fundamental." Even today, when society's views on abortion are changing, the very existence of the debate is evidence that the "right" to an abortion is not so universally accepted as [Roe] would have us believe.

To reach its result the Court necessarily has had to find within the scope of the Fourteenth Amendment a right that was apparently completely unknown to the drafters of the Amendment. As early as 1821, the first state law dealing directly with abortion was enacted by the Connecticut Legislature. By the time of the adoption of the Fourteenth Amendment in 1868, there were at least 36 laws enacted by state or territorial legislatures limiting abortion. While many States have amended or updated their laws, 21 of the laws on the books in 1868 remain in effect today. Indeed, the Texas statute struck down today was, as the majority notes, first enacted in 1857 and "has remained substantially unchanged to the present time."

There apparently was no question concerning the validity of this provision or of any of the other state statutes when the Fourteenth Amendment was adopted. The only conclusion possible from this history is that the drafters did not intend to have the Fourteenth Amendment withdraw from the States the power to legislate with respect to this matter.

Even if one were to agree that the case that the Court decides were here, and that the enunciation of the substantive constitutional law in the Court's opinion were proper, the actual disposition of the case by the Court is still difficult to justify. The Texas statute is struck down in toto, even though the Court apparently concedes that at later periods of pregnancy Texas might impose these selfsame statutory limitations on abortion. My understanding of past practice is that a statute found to be invalid as applied to a particular plaintiff, but not unconstitutional as a whole, is not simply "struck down" but is, instead, declared unconstitutional as applied to the fact situation before the Court.

For all of the foregoing reasons, I respectfully dissent.

DOE v. BOLTON

EXCERPTS

"It would be physically and emotionally damaging to Doe to bring a child into her poor "fatherless" family, and . . . advances in medicine and medical techniques have made it safer for a woman to have a medically induced abortion than for her to bear a child."

"This is not to say that Georgia may not or should not, from and after the end of the first trimester, adopt standards for licensing all facilities where abortions may be performed so long as those standards are legitimately related to the objective the State seeks to accomplish."

Justice Harry Blackmun

In Brief

Question: Is the Georgia criminal abortion law
                 constitutional?

Lower Court: U.S. District Court, Northern Georgia

Law: Georgia Criminal Code, Sections 26-1201-3

Parties: Mary Doe, pseudonym of Sandra Race Cano
                 Arthur Bolton, Georgia Attorney General

Counsel: For Doe: Margie Pitts Hames
                 For Bolton: Dorothy Beasley

Arguments: December 13, 1971; October 11, 1972

Decision: January 22, 1973

Majority: Chief Justice Burger, Justices Douglas, Brennan,
                 Stewart, Marshall, Blackmun, Powell

Minority: Justices White, Rehnquist

Decision by: Justice Blackmun (p. 59)

Concurrences: Chief Justice Burger (see *Roe*, p. 34)
                 Justice Douglas (see *Roe*, p. 35)

Dissents: Justice White (see *Roe*, p. 47)
                 Justice Rehnquist (see *Roe*, p. 49)

Official Text: U.S. Reports, Vol. 410, p. 179
Lower Court: Federal Supplement, Vol. 319, p. 1048

THE DOE COURT

Chief Justice Warren Burger
Appointed 1969 by Richard M. Nixon

Associate Justice William O. Douglas
Appointed 1939 by Franklin D. Roosevelt

Associate Justice William Brennan
Appointed 1956 by Dwight D. Eisenhower

Associate Justice Potter Stewart
Appointed 1958 by Dwight D. Eisenhower

Associate Justice Byron White
Appointed 1962 by John F. Kennedy

Associate Justice Thurgood Marshall
Appointed 1967 by Lyndon B. Johnson

Associate Justice Harry Blackmun
Appointed 1970 by Richard M. Nixon

Associate Justice Lewis Powell
Appointed 1972 by Richard M. Nixon

Associate Justice William Rehnquist
Appointed 1971 by Richard M. Nixon

DOE v. BOLTON

January 22, 1973

JUSTICE BLACKMUN: In this appeal, the criminal abortion statutes recently enacted in Georgia are challenged on constitutional grounds. The statutes are Sections 26-1201 through 26-1203 of the State's Criminal Code. In *Roe v. Wade*, we today have struck down, as constitutionally defective, the Texas criminal abortion statutes that are representative of provisions long in effect in a majority of our States. The Georgia legislation, however, is different and merits separate consideration.

... [T]he 1968 statutes are patterned upon the American Law Institute's Model Penal Code. ... The ALI proposal has served as the model for recent legislation in approximately one-fourth of our States. The new Georgia provisions replaced statutory law that had been in effect for more than 90 years. The predecessor statute paralleled the Texas legislation considered in *Roe v. Wade*, and made all abortions criminal except those necessary "to preserve the life" of the pregnant woman. The new statutes have not been tested on constitutional grounds in the Georgia state courts.

Section 26-1201, with a referenced exception, makes abortion a crime, and Section 26-1203 provides that a person convicted of that crime shall be punished by imprisonment for not less than one nor more than 10 years. Section 26-1202(a) ... removes from Section 1201's definition of criminal abortion, and thus makes noncriminal, an abortion "performed by a physician duly licensed" in Georgia when, "based upon his best clinical judgment ... an abortion is necessary because:

"(1) A continuation of the pregnancy would endanger
the life of the pregnant woman or would seriously and
permanently injure her health; or

"(2) The fetus would very likely be born with a grave,
permanent, and irremediable mental or physical defect;
or

"(3) The pregnancy resulted from forcible or statutory
rape."

Section 26-1202 also requires . . . that, for an abortion to
be authorized or performed as a non-criminal procedure,
additional conditions must be fulfilled. These are (1) and
(2) residence of the woman in Georgia; (3) reduction to
writing of the performing physician's medical judgment
that an abortion is justified for one or more of the reasons
specified by Section 26-1202(a), with written concurrence
in that judgment by at least two other Georgia-licensed
physicians, based upon their separate personal medical examinations of the woman; (4) performance of the abortion in a hospital licensed by the State Board of Health
and also accredited by the Joint Commission on Accreditation of Hospitals; (5) advance approval by an abortion
committee of not less than three members of the
hospital's staff; (6) certifications in a rape situation; and
(7), (8), and (9) maintenance and confidentiality of records. There is a provision . . . for judicial determination
of the legality of a proposed abortion on petition of the
judicial circuit law officer or of a close relative . . . of the
unborn child, and for expeditious hearing of that petition.
There is also a provision . . . giving a hospital the right not
to admit an abortion patient and giving any physician and
any hospital employee or staff member the right, on moral or religious grounds, not to participate in the procedure.

On April 16, 1970, Mary Doe, 23 other individuals (nine described as Georgia-licensed physicians, seven as nurses registered in the State, five as clergymen, and two as social workers), and two nonprofit Georgia corporations that advocate abortion reform instituted this federal action in the Northern District of Georgia against the State's attorney general, the district attorney of Fulton County, and the chief of police of the city of Atlanta. [Doe] sought a [ruling by the court] that the Georgia abortion statutes were unconstitutional in their entirety. [Doe] also sought [to restrain] the [state, county, and city officials] from enforcing the statutes.

Mary Doe alleged:

(1) She was a 22-year-old Georgia citizen, married, and nine weeks pregnant. She had three living children. The two older ones had been placed in a foster home because of Doe's poverty and inability to care for them. The youngest, born July 19, 1969, had been placed for adoption. Her husband had recently abandoned her and she was forced to live with her indigent parents and their eight children. She and her husband, however, had become reconciled. He was a construction worker employed only sporadically. She had been a mental patient at the State Hospital. She had been advised that an abortion could be performed on her with less danger to her health than if she gave birth to the child she was carrying. She would be unable to care for or support the new child.

On March 25, 1970, she applied to the Abortion Committee of Grady Memorial Hospital, Atlanta, for a therapeutic abortion under Section 26-1202. Her application was denied 16 days later, on April 10, when she was eight weeks pregnant, on the ground that her situation was not one described in Section 26-1202(a).

(3) Because her application was denied, she was forced either to relinquish "her right to decide when and how many children she will bear" or to seek an abortion that was illegal under the Georgia statutes. This invaded her rights of privacy and liberty in matters related to family, marriage, and sex, and deprived her of the right to choose whether to bear children. This was a violation of rights guaranteed her by the First, Fourth, Fifth, Ninth, and Fourteenth Amendments. The statutes also denied her equal protection and procedural due process and, because they were unconstitutionally vague, deterred hospitals and doctors from performing abortions. She sued "on her own behalf and on behalf of all others similarly situated."

The other plaintiffs [doctors, nurses, clergy, and social workers] alleged that the Georgia statutes "chilled and deterred" them from practicing their respective professions and deprived them of rights guaranteed by the First, Fourth, and Fourteenth Amendments. . . .

The District Court . . . concluded that the limitation in the Georgia statute of the "number of reasons for which an abortion may be sought" improperly restricted Doe's rights of privacy articulated in *Griswold v. Connecticut,* and of "personal liberty," both of which it thought "broad enough to include the decision to abort a pregnancy." As a consequence, the court held invalid those portions of Sections 26-1202(a) and (b)(3) limiting legal abortions to the three situations specified; Section 26-1202(b)(6) relating to certifications in a rape situation; and Section 26-1202(c) authorizing a court test. . . . The court, however, held that Georgia's interest in protection of health, and the existence of a "*potential* of independent human existence," justified state regulation of "the manner of performance as well as the quality of the final decision to abort," and it refused to strike down the other provisions of the statutes. It denied the request for an injunction [court order stopping an action].

. . . . Our decision in *Roe v. Wade* establishes (1) that, despite her pseudonym, we may accept as true, for this case, Mary Doe's existence and her pregnant state on April 16, 1970; (2) that the constitutional issue is substantial; (3) that the interim termination of Doe's and all other Georgia pregnancies in existence in 1970 has not rendered the case moot [already decided]; and (4) that Doe . . . has [the right to bring this matter to court].

. . . . We conclude . . . that the physician-appellants, who are Georgia-licensed doctors consulted by pregnant women, also present a justiciable controversy and do have standing despite the fact that the record does not disclose that any one of them has been prosecuted, or threatened with prosecution, for violation of the State's abortion statutes. The physician is the one against whom these criminal statutes directly operate in the event he procures an abortion that does not meet the statutory exceptions and conditions. . . . [He] should not be required to await and undergo a criminal prosecution as the sole means of seeking relief.

. . . . We conclude that we need not pass upon the status of [the nurses, clergy, social workers, and corporations], for the issues are sufficiently and adequately presented by Doe and the physician-appellants. . . .

[Doe] attack[s] on several grounds those portions of the Georgia abortion statutes that remain after the District Court decision: undue restriction of a right to personal and marital privacy; vagueness; deprivation of substantive and procedural due process; improper restriction to Georgia residents; and denial of equal protection.

Roe v. Wade sets forth our conclusion that a pregnant woman does not have an absolute constitutional right to an abortion on her demand. What is said there is applicable here and need not be repeated.

[Doe] go[es] on to argue, however, that the present Georgia statutes must be viewed historically, that is, from the fact that prior to the 1968 Act an abortion in Georgia was not criminal if performed to "preserve the life" of the mother. It is suggested that the present statute, as well, has this emphasis on the mother's rights, not on those of the fetus. . . .

[Doe] then argue[s] that the statutes do not adequately protect the woman's right. This is so because it would be physically and emotionally damaging to Doe to bring a child into her poor "fatherless" family, and because advances in medicine and medical techniques have made it safer for a woman to have a medically induced abortion than for her to bear a child. Thus, "a statute that requires a woman to carry an unwanted pregnancy to term infringes not only on a fundamental right of privacy but on the right to life itself."

[Doe] recognize[s] that a century ago medical knowledge was not so advanced as it is today, that the techniques of antisepsis were not known, and that any abortion procedure was dangerous for the woman. To restrict the legality of the abortion to the situation where it was deemed necessary, in medical judgment, for the preservation of the woman's life was only a natural conclusion in the exercise of the legislative judgment of that time. A State is not to be reproached, however, for a past judgmental determination made in the light of then-existing medical knowledge. It is perhaps unfair to argue . . . that because the early focus was on the preservation of the woman's life, the State's present professed interest in the protection of embryonic and fetal life is to be downgraded. That argument denies the State the right to readjust its views and emphases in the light of the advanced knowledge and techniques of the day.

[Doe] argue[s] that Section 26-1202(a) of the Georgia statutes, as it has been left by the District Court's decision, is unconstitutionally vague. This argument centers on the proposition that, with the District Court's having stricken the statutorily specified reasons, it still remains a crime for a physician to perform an abortion except when, as Section 26-1202(a) reads, it is "based upon his best clinical judgment that an abortion is necessary." The appellants contend that the word "necessary" does not warn the physician of what conduct is proscribed; that the statute is wholly without objective standards and is subject to diverse interpretation; and that doctors will choose to err on the side of caution and will be arbitrary.

The net result of the District Court's decision is that the abortion determination, so far as the physician is concerned, is made in the exercise of his professional, that is, his "best clinical," judgment in the light of *all* the attendant circumstances. He is not now restricted to the three situations originally specified. Instead, he may range farther afield wherever his medical judgment, properly and professionally exercised, so dictates and directs him.

The vagueness argument is set at rest by the decision in *United States v. Vuitch*, where the issue was raised with respect to a District of Columbia statute making abortions criminal "unless the same were done as necessary for the preservation of the mother's life or health and under the direction of a competent licensed practitioner of medicine." That statute has been construed to bear upon psychological as well as physical well-being. This being so, the Court concluded that the term "health" presented no problem of vagueness. "Indeed, whether a particular operation is necessary for a patient's physical or mental health is a judgment that physicians are obviously called upon to make routinely whenever surgery is considered." This conclusion is equally applicable here. Whether, in the words of the Georgia statute, "an abortion is necessary" is a professional judgment that the Georgia physician will be called upon to make routinely.

We agree with the District Court that the medical judgment may be exercised in the light of all factors - physical, emotional, psychological, familial, and the woman's age - relevant to the well-being of the patient. All these factors may relate to health. This allows the attending physician the room he needs to make his best medical judgment. And it is room that operates for the benefit, not the disadvantage, of the pregnant woman.

[Doe] next argue[s] that the District Court should have declared unconstitutional three procedural demands of the Georgia statute: (1) that the abortion be performed in a hospital accredited by the Joint Commission on Accreditation of Hospitals; (2) that the procedure be approved by the hospital staff abortion committee; and (3) that the performing physician's judgment be confirmed by the independent examinations of the patient by two other licensed physicians. [Doe] attack[s] these provisions not only on the ground that they unduly restrict the woman's right of privacy, but also on procedural due process and equal protection grounds. The physician-appellants also argue that, by subjecting a doctor's individual medical judgment to committee approval and to confirming consultations, the statute impermissibly restricts the physician's right to practice his profession and deprives him of due process.

The Joint Commission on Accreditation of Hospitals is an organization without governmental sponsorship or overtones. No question whatever is raised concerning the integrity of the organization or the high purpose of the accreditation process. That process, however, has to do with hospital standards generally and has no present particularized concern with abortion as a medical or surgical procedure. In Georgia, there is no restriction on the performance of nonabortion surgery in a hospital not yet accredited by the JCAH so long as other requirements imposed by the State, such as licensing of the hospital and of the operating surgeon, are met. Furthermore, accreditation by the Commission is not granted until a hospital has been in operation at least one year. The Model Penal Code . . . contains no requirement for JCAH accreditation. And the Uniform Abortion Act, approved by the American Bar Association in February 1972, contains no JCAH-accredited hospital specification. Some courts have held that a JCAH-accreditation requirement is an overbroad infringement of fundamental rights because it does not relate to the particular medical problems and dangers of the abortion operation.

We hold that the JCAH-accreditation requirement does not withstand constitutional scrutiny in the present context. It is a requirement that simply is not "based on differences that are reasonably related to the purposes of the Act in which it is found."

This is not to say that Georgia may not or should not, from and after the end of the first trimester, adopt standards for licensing all facilities where abortions may be performed so long as those standards are legitimately related to the objective the State seeks to accomplish. . . . [Doe has] presented us with a mass of data purporting to demonstrate that some facilities other than hospitals are entirely adequate to perform abortions. . . . The State, on the other hand, has not presented persuasive data to show that only hospitals meet its acknowledged interest in insuring the quality of the operation and the full protection of the patient. We feel compelled to agree with [Doe] that the State must show more than it has in order to prove that only the full resources of a licensed hospital, rather than those of some other appropriately licensed institution, satisfy these health interests. We hold that the hospital requirement of the Georgia law, because it fails to exclude the first trimester of pregnancy, is also invalid. In so holding we naturally express no opinion on the medical judgment involved in any particular case, that is, whether the patient's situation is such than an abortion should be performed in a hospital, rather than in some other facility.

. . . . Doe . . . argues that she was denied due process because she could not make a presentation to the committee. It is not clear from the record, however, whether Doe's own consulting physician was or was not a member of the committee or did or did not present her case, or, indeed, whether she herself was or was not there. We see nothing in the Georgia statute that explicitly denies access to the committee by or on behalf of the woman. If the access point alone were involved, we would not be persuaded to strike down the committee provision on the unsupported assumption that access is not provided.

[Doe] attack[s] the discretion the statute leaves to the committee. The most concrete argument ... advance[d] is [the] suggestion that it is still a badge of infamy "in many minds" to bear an illegitimate child, and that the Georgia system enables the committee members' personal views as to extramarital sex relations, and punishment therefor, to govern their decisions. This approach obviously is one founded on suspicion and one that discloses a lack of confidence in the integrity of physicians. To say that physicians will be guided in their hospital committee decisions by their predilections on extramarital sex unduly narrows the issue to pregnancy outside marriage. (Doe's own situation did not involve extramarital sex and its product.) [Doe's] suggestion is necessarily somewhat degrading to the conscientious physician, particularly the obstetrician, whose professional activity is concerned with the physical and mental welfare, the woes, the emotions, and the concern of his female patients. He, perhaps more than anyone else, is knowledgeable in this area of patient care, and he is aware of human frailty, so-called "error," and needs. The good physician - despite the presence of rascals in the medical profession, as in all others, we trust that most physicians are "good" - will have a sympathy and an understanding for the pregnant patient that probably is not exceeded by those who participate in other areas of professional counseling.

It is perhaps worth nothing that the abortion committee has a function of its own. It is a committee of the hospital and it is composed of members of the institution's medical staff. The membership usually is a changing one. In this way, its work burden is shared and is more readily accepted. The committee's function is protective. It enables the hospital appropriately to be advised that its posture and activities are in accord with legal requirements. It is to be remembered that the hospital is an entity and that it, too, has legal rights and legal obligations.

Saying all this, however, does not settle the issue of the constitutional propriety of the committee requirement. Viewing the Georgia statute as a whole, we see no constitutionally justifiable pertinence in the structure for the advance approval by the abortion committee. With regard to the protection of potential life, the medical judgment is already completed prior to the committee stage, and review by a committee once removed from diagnosis is basically redundant. We are not cited to any other surgical procedure made subject to committee approval as a matter of state criminal law. The woman's right to receive medical care in accordance with her licensed physician's best judgment and the physician's right to administer it are substantially limited by this statutorily imposed overview. And the hospital itself is otherwise fully protected. Under Section 26-1202(e), the hospital is free not to admit a patient for an abortion. It is even free not to have an abortion committee. Further, a physician or any other employee has the right to refrain, for moral or religious reasons, from participating in the abortion procedure. These provisions obviously are in the statute in order to afford appropriate protection to the individual and to the denominational hospital. Section 26-1202(e) affords adequate protection to the hospital, and little more is provided by the committee prescribed by Section 26-1202(b)(5).

We conclude that the interposition of the hospital abortion committee is unduly restrictive of the patient's rights and needs that, at this point, have already been medically delineated and substantiated by her personal physician. To ask more serves neither the hospital nor the State.

The third aspect of [Doe's] attack centers on the "time and availability of adequate medical facilities and personnel." It is said that the system imposes substantial and irrational roadblocks and "is patently unsuited" to prompt determination of the abortion decision. Time, of course, is critical in abortion. Risks during the first trimester of pregnancy are admittedly lower than during later months.

[Doe] purport[s] to show by a local study of Grady Memorial Hospital (serving indigent residents in Fulton and DeKalb Counties) that the "mechanics of the system itself forced . . . discontinuance of the abortion process" because the median time for the workup was 15 days. The same study shows, however, that 27% of the candidates for abortion were already 13 or more weeks pregnant at the time of application, that is, they were at the end of or beyond the first trimester when they made their applications. It is too much to say . . . that these particular persons "were victims of a system over which they [had] no control." If higher risk was incurred because of abortions in the second rather than the first trimester, much of that risk was due to delay in application, and not to the alleged cumbersomeness of the system. We note, in passing, that . . . Doe had no delay problem herself; the decision in her case was made well within the first trimester.

. . . . There remains . . . the required confirmation by two Georgia-licensed physicians in addition to the recommendation of the pregnant woman's own consultant (making under the statute, a total of six physicians involved, including the three on the hospital's abortion committee). We conclude that this provision, too, must fall.

The statute's emphasis, as has been repetitively noted, is on the attending physician's "best clinical judgment that an abortion is necessary." That should be sufficient. The reasons for the presence of the confirmation step in the statute are perhaps apparent, but they are insufficient to withstand constitutional challenge. Again, no other voluntary medical or surgical procedure for which Georgia requires confirmation by two other physicians has been cited to us. If a physician is licensed by the State, he is recognized by the State as capable of exercising acceptable clinical judgment. If he fails in this, professional censure and deprivation of his license are available remedies. Required acquiescence by co-practitioners has no rational connection with a patient's needs and unduly infringes on the physician's right to practice. The attending physician will know when a consultation is advisable - the doubtful situation, the need for assurance when the medical decision is a delicate one, and the like. Physicians have followed this routine historically and know its usefulness and benefit for all concerned. It is still true today that "[r]eliance must be placed upon the assurance given by his license, issued by an authority competent to judge in that respect, that he [the physician] possesses the requisite qualifications."

[Doe] attack[s] the residency requirement of the Georgia law . . . as violative of the right to travel stressed in *Shapiro v. Thompson* and other cases. A requirement of this kind, of course, could be deemed to have some relationship to the availability of post-procedure medical care for the aborted patient.

Nevertheless, we do not uphold the constitutionality of the residence requirement. It is not based on any policy of preserving state-supported facilities for Georgia residents, for the bar also applies to private hospitals and to privately retained physicians. There is no intimation, either, that Georgia facilities are utilized to capacity in caring for Georgia residents. Just as the Privileges and Immunities Clause [of the Constitution] protects persons who enter other States to ply their trade, so must it protect persons who enter Georgia seeking the medical services that are available there. A contrary holding would mean that a State could limit to its own residents the general medical care available within its borders. This we could not approve.

The last argument on this phase of the case is one that often is made, namely, that the Georgia system is violative of equal protection because it discriminates against the poor. [Doe] do[es] not urge that abortions should be performed by persons other than licensed physicians, so we have no argument that because the wealthy can better afford physicians, the poor should have nonphysicians made available to them. [Doe] acknowledged that the procedures are "nondiscriminatory in . . . express terms" but . . . suggest[s] that they have produced invidious discrimination[s, resting] . . . primarily on the accreditation and approval and confirmation requirements, . . . and on the assertion that most of Georgia's counties have no accredited hospital. We have set aside the accreditation, approval, and confirmation requirements, however, and with that, the discrimination argument collapses in all significant aspects.

. . . . We assume that Georgia's prosecutorial authorities will give full recognition to the judgment of this Court.

In summary, we hold that the JCAH-accredited hospital provision and the requirements as to approval by the hospital abortion committee, as to confirmation by two independent physicians, and as to residence in Georgia are all violative of the Fourteenth Amendment. . . .

The judgment of the District Court is modified accordingly and, as so modified, is affirmed. . . .

CHIEF JUSTICE BURGER concurred. [See the opinion in *Roe v. Wade*, p. 34.]

JUSTICE DOUGLAS concurred. [See the opinion in *Roe v. Wade*, p. 35.]

JUSTICE WHITE (joined by Justice Rehnquist) dissented. [See the opinion in *Roe v. Wade*, p. 47.]

PLANNED PARENTHOOD
v. DANFORTH

EXCERPTS

"[T]he State does not have the constitutional authority to give a third party an absolute, and possibly arbitrary, veto over the decision of the physician and his patient to terminate the patient's pregnancy, regardless of the reason for withholding the consent."

Justice Harry Blackmun

"That is a grave decision, and a girl of tender years, under emotional stress, may be ill-equipped to make it without mature advice and emotional support."

Justice Potter Stewart

"A father's interest in having a child - perhaps his only child - may be unmatched by any other interest in his life. It is truly surprising that the majority finds in the United States Constitution . . . a rule that the State must assign a greater value to a mother's decision to cut off a potential human life by abortion than to a father's decision to let it mature into a live child."

Justice Byron White

In Brief

Question: Is the Missouri Abortion Law constitutional?

Lower Court: U.S. District Court, Eastern Missouri

Law: Missouri Abortion Act of June 14, 1974

Parties: Planned Parenthood of Central Missouri
              John Danforth, Missouri Attorney General

Counsel: For Planned Parenthood: Frank Susman
              For Missouri: John Danforth

Arguments: March 23, 1976

Decision: July 1, 1976

Majority: Justices Brennan, Stewart, Marshall, Blackmun, Powell

Minority: Chief Justice Burger, Justices White, Rehnquist, Stevens

Decision by: Justice Blackmun (p. 79)

Concurrence: Justice Stewart (p. 94)

Concurrences in part/Dissents in part:

                 Justice White (p. 95)
                 Justice Stevens (p. 100)

Offical Text: U.S. Reports, Vol. 428, p. 52
Lower Court: Federal Supplement, Vol. 392, p. 1362

THE DANFORTH COURT

Chief Justice Warren Burger
Appointed 1969 by Richard M. Nixon

Associate Justice William Brennan
Appointed 1956 by Dwight D. Eisenhower

Associate Justice Potter Stewart
Appointed 1958 by Dwight D. Eisenhower

Associate Justice Byron White
Appointed 1962 by John F. Kennedy

Associate Justice Thurgood Marshall
Appointed 1967 by Lyndon B. Johnson

Associate Justice Harry Blackmun
Appointed 1970 by Richard M. Nixon

Associate Justice Lewis Powell
Appointed 1972 by Richard M. Nixon

Associate Justice William Rehnquist
Appointed 1971 by Richard M. Nixon

Associate Justice John Paul Stevens
Appointed 1975 by Gerald R. Ford

PLANNED PARENTHOOD
v. DANFORTH

July 1, 1976

JUSTICE BLACKMUN: This case is a logical and anticipated corollary to *Roe v. Wade* and *Doe v. Bolton*, for it
raises issues secondary to those that were then before the
Court. Indeed, some of the questions now presented were
forecast and reserved [set aside] in *Roe* and *Doe*.

. . . . In June 1974, somewhat more than a year after *Roe*
and *Doe* had been decided, Missouri's 77th General Assembly, in its Second Regular Session, enacted House
Committee Substitute for House Bill No. 1211
(hereinafter Act). The legislation was approved by the
Governor on June 14, 1974, and became effective immediately by reason of an emergency clause. . . . The Act . . .
imposes a structure for the control and regulation of abortions in Missouri during all stages of pregnancy.

Three days after the Act became effective, the present
litigation was instituted in the United States District
Court for the Eastern District of Missouri. The plaintiffs
are Planned Parenthood of Central Missouri, a not-for-
profit Missouri corporation which maintains a facility in
Columbia, Missouri, for the performance of abortions; David Hall, M.D.; and Michael Freiman, M.D. . . .

The named defendants are the Attorney General of Missouri and the Circuit Attorney of the city of St. Louis "in
his representative capacity" and "as the representative of
the class of all similar Prosecuting Attorneys of the various counties of the State of Missouri."

[Planned Parenthood] brought the action on [its] own behalf and, purportedly, "on behalf of the entire class consisting of duly licensed physicians and surgeons presently performing or desiring to perform the termination of pregnancies and on behalf of the entire class consisting of their patients desiring the termination of pregnancy, all within the State of Missouri." [Planned Parenthood] sought . . . to enjoin [stop] enforcement of the Act on the ground, among others, that certain of its provisions deprived them and their patients of various constitutional rights: "the right to privacy in the physician-patient relationship"; the physicians' "right to practice medicine according to the highest standards of medical practice"; the female patients' right to determine whether to bear children; the patients' "right to life due to the inherent risk involved in childbirth" or in medical procedures alternative to abortion; the physicians' "right to give and . . . patients' right to receive safe and adequate medical advice and treatment, pertaining to the decision of whether to carry a given pregnancy to term and the method of termination"; the patients' right under the Eighth Amendment to be free from cruel and unusual punishment "by forcing and coercing them to bear each pregnancy they conceive"; and, by being placed "in the position of decision making beset with . . . inherent possibilities of bias and conflict of interest," the physician's right to due process of law guaranteed by the Fourteenth Amendment.

The particular provisions of the Act that remained under specific challenge at the end of trial were Section 2(2), defining the term "viability"; Section 3(2), requiring from the woman, prior to submitting to abortion during the first 12 weeks of pregnancy, a certification in writing that she consents to the procedure and "that her consent is informed and freely given and is not the result of coercion";

Section 3(3), requiring, for the same period, "the written consent of the woman's spouse, unless the abortion is certified by a licensed physician to be necessary in order to preserve the life of the mother"; Section 3(4), requiring, for the same period, "the written consent of one parent or person in loco parentis [in place of the parent] of the woman if the woman is unmarried and under the age of eighteen years, unless the abortion is certified by a licensed physician as necessary in order to preserve the life of the mother"; Section 6(1), requiring the physician to exercise professional care "to preserve the life and health of the fetus" and, failing such, deeming him guilty of manslaughter . . . ; Section 7, declaring an infant, who survives "an attempted abortion which was not performed to save the life or health of the mother," to be "an abandoned ward of the state under the jurisdiction of the juvenile court," and depriving the mother, and also the father if he consented to the abortion, of parental rights; Section 9, the legislative finding that method of abortion known as saline amniocentesis "is deleterious to maternal health," and prohibiting that method after the first 12 weeks of pregnancy; and Sections 10 and 11, imposing reporting and maintenance of record requirements for health facilities and for physicians who perform abortions.

The case was presented to a three-judge District Court. . . .

On the issues as to the constitutionality of the several challenged sections of the Act, the District Court, largely by a divided vote, ruled that all except the first sentence of Section 6(1) withstood the attack. That sentence was held to be constitutionally impermissible because it imposed upon the physician the duty to exercise at all stages of pregnancy "that degree of professional skill, care and diligence to preserve the life and health of the fetus" that

"would be required . . . to preserve the life and health of
any fetus intended to be born." Inasmuch as this failed to
exclude the stage of pregnancy prior to viability, the provision was "unconstitutionally overbroad."

. . . . In *Roe v. Wade* the Court concluded that the "right
of privacy, whether it be founded in the Fourteenth
Amendment's concept of personal liberty and restrictions
upon state action, as we feel it is, or, as the District Court
determined, in the Ninth Amendment's reservation of
rights to the people, is broad enough to encompass a woman's decision whether or not to terminate her pregnancy."
It emphatically rejected, however, the proferred argument "that the woman's right is absolute and that she is
entitled to terminate her pregnancy at whatever time, in
whatever way, and for whatever reason she alone
chooses." Instead, this right "must be considered against
important state interests in regulation."

The Court went on to say that the "pregnant woman cannot be isolated in her privacy," for she "carries an embryo
and, later, a fetus." It was therefore "reasonable and appropriate for a State to decide that at some point in time
another interest, that of health of the mother or that of
potential human life, becomes significantly involved. The
woman's privacy is no longer sole and any right of privacy she possesses must be measured accordingly. The
Court stressed the measure of the State's interest in "the
light of present medical knowledge." It concluded that
the permissibility of state regulation was to be viewed in
three stages: "For the stage prior to approximately the end
of the first trimester, the abortion decision and its effectuation must be left to the medical judgment of the pregnant woman's attending physician," without interference
from the State. The participation by the attending physi-

cian in the abortion decision, and his responsibility in that decision, thus, were emphasized. After the first stage, as so described, the State may, if it chooses, reasonably regulate the abortion procedure to preserve and protect maternal health. Finally, for the stage subsequent to viability, a point purposefully left flexible for professional determination, and dependent upon developing medical skill and technical ability, the State may regulate an abortion to protect the life of the fetus and even may proscribe abortion except where it is necessary, in appropriate medical judgment, for the preservation of the life or health of the mother.

. . . . Our primary task . . . is to consider each of the challenged provisions of the new Missouri abortion statute in the particular light of the opinions and decisions in *Roe* and in *Doe*. . . . To this we now turn. . . .

The definition of viability. Section 2(2) of the Act defines "viability" as "that stage of fetal development when the life of the unborn child may be continued indefinitely outside the womb by natural or artificial life-supportive systems." [Planned Parenthood] claim[s] that this definition violates and conflicts with the discussion of viability in our opinion in *Roe*. In particular, [they] object to the failure of the definition to contain any reference to a gestational time period, to its failure to incorporate and reflect the three stages of pregnancy, to the presence of the word "indefinitely," and to the extra burden of regulation imposed. It is suggested that the definition expands the Court's definition of viability, as expressed in *Roe*, and amounts to a legislative determination of what is properly a matter for medical judgment. It is said that the "mere possibility of momentary survival is not the medical standard of viability."

In *Roe*, we used the term "viable," properly we thought, to signify the point at which the fetus is "potentially able to live outside the mother's womb, albeit with artificial aid," and presumably capable of "meaningful life outside the mother's womb." We noted that this point "is usually placed" at about seven months or 28 weeks, but may occur earlier.

We agree with the District Court and conclude that the definition of viability in the Act does not conflict with what was said and held in *Roe*. . . .

[W]e agree with the District Court that it is not the proper function of the legislature or the courts to place viability, which essentially is a medical concept, at a specific point in the gestation period. The time when viability is achieved may vary with each pregnancy, and the determination of whether a particular fetus is viable is, and must be, a matter for the judgment of the responsible attending physician. . . .

. . . . We . . . hold that the Act's definition of "viability" comports with *Roe* and withstands the constitutional attack made upon it in this litigation.

The woman's consent. Under Section 3(2) of the Act, a woman, prior to submitting to an abortion during the first 12 weeks of pregnancy, must certify in writing her consent to the procedure and "that her consent is informed and freely given and is not the result of coercion." [Planned Parenthood] argue[s] that this requirement is violative of *Roe v. Wade*. . . .

[T]he imposition by Section 3(2) of such a requirement for termination of pregnancy even during the first stage, in our view, is not in itself an unconstitutional requirement. The decision to abort, indeed, is an important, and often a stressful one, and it is desirable and imperative that it be made with full knowledge of its nature and consequences. The woman is the one primarily concerned, and her awareness of the decision and its significance may be assured, constitutionally, by the State to the extent of requiring her prior written consent.

We could not say that a requirement imposed by the State that a prior written consent for any surgery would be unconstitutional. As a consequence, we see no constitutional defect in requiring it only for some types of surgery as, for example, an intracardiac procedure, or where the surgical risk is elevated above a specified mortality level, or, for that matter, for abortions.

The spouse's consent. Section 3(3) requires the prior written consent of the spouse of the woman seeking an abortion during the first 12 weeks of pregnancy, unless "the abortion is certified by a licensed physician to be necessary in order to preserve the life of the mother."

[Danforth] defend[s] Section 3(3) on the ground that it was enacted in the light of the General Assembly's "perception of marriage as an institution," and that any major change in family status is a decision to be made jointly by the marriage partners. . . .

[Planned Parenthood], on the other hand, contend[s] that Section 3(3) obviously is designed to afford the husband the right unilaterally to prevent or veto an abortion, whether or not he is the father of the fetus, and that this not only violates *Roe* and *Doe* but is also in conflict with other decided cases. . . .

In *Roe* and *Doe* we specifically reserved [set aside] decision on the question whether a requirement for consent by the father of the fetus, by the spouse, or by the parents, or a parent, of an unmarried minor, may be constitutionally imposed. We now hold that the State may not constitutionally require the consent of the spouse, as is specified under Section 3(3) of the Missouri Act, as a condition for abortion during the first 12 weeks of pregnancy. . . .

We are not unaware of the deep and proper concern and interest that a devoted and protective husband has in his wife's pregnancy and in the growth and development of the fetus she is carrying. Neither has this Court failed to appreciate the importance of the marital relationship in our society. Moreover, we recognize that the decision whether to undergo or to forgo an abortion may have profound effects on the future of any marriage, effects that are both physical and mental, and possibly deleterious. Notwithstanding these factors, we cannot hold that the State has the constitutional authority to give the spouse unilaterally the ability to prohibit the wife from terminating her pregnancy, when the State itself lacks that right.

. . . . We recognize, of course, that when a woman, with the approval of her physician but without the approval of her husband, decides to terminate her pregnancy, it could be said that she is acting unilaterally. The obvious fact is that when the wife and the husband disagree on this decision, the view of only one of the two marriage partners can prevail. Inasmuch as it is the woman who physically bears the child and who is the more directly and immediately affected by the pregnancy, as between the two, the balance weighs in her favor.

We conclude that Section 3(3) of the Missouri Act is inconsistent with the standards enunciated in *Roe v. Wade*, and is unconstitutional. . . .

Parental consent. Section 3(4) requires, with respect to the first 12 weeks of pregnancy, where the woman is unmarried and under the age of 18 years, the written consent of a parent or person in loco parentis [in place of the parent] unless, again, "the abortion is certified by a licensed physician as necessary in order to preserve the life of the mother." It is to be observed that only one parent need consent.

[Danforth] defend[s] the statute in several ways[, pointing] out that the law properly may subject minors to more stringent limitations than are permissible with respect to adults. . . .

[Planned Parenthood] . . . emphasize[s] that no other Missouri statute specifically requires the additional consent of a minor's parent for medical or surgical treatment, and that in Missouri a minor legally may consent to medical services for pregnancy (excluding abortion), venereal disease, and drug abuse. . . .

We agree with [Planned Parenthood] . . . that the State may not impose a blanket provision, such as Section 3(4), requiring the consent of a parent or person [in place of the parent] as a condition for abortion of an unmarried minor during the first 12 weeks of her pregnancy. Just as with the requirement of consent from the spouse, so here, the State does not have the constitutional authority to give a third party an absolute, and possibly arbitrary, veto over the decision of the physician and his patient to terminate

the patient's pregnancy, regardless of the reason for withholding the consent.

Constitutional rights do not mature and come into being
magically only when one attains the state-defined age of
majority. Minors, as well as adults, are protected by the
Constitution and possess constitutional rights. The Court
indeed, however, long has recognized that the State has
somewhat broader authority to regulate the activities of
children than of adults. It remains, then, to examine
whether there is any significant state interest in condition-
ing an abortion on the consent of a parent or person [in
place of the parent] that is not present in the case of an
adult.

One suggested interest is the safeguarding of the family
unit and of parental authority. It is difficult, however, to
conclude that providing a parent with absolute power to
overrule a determination, made by the physician and his
minor patient, to terminate the patient's pregnancy will
serve to strengthen the family unit. Neither is it likely
that such veto power will enhance parental authority or
control where the minor and the non-consenting parent
are so fundamentally in conflict and the very existence of
the pregnancy already has fractured the family structure.
Any independent interest the parent may have in the termination of the minor daughter's pregnancy is no more
weighty than the right of privacy of the competent minor
mature enough to have become pregnant.

We emphasize that our holding that Section 3(4) is invalid
does not suggest that every minor, regardless of age or
maturity, may give effective consent for termination of
her pregnancy. The fault with Section 3(4) is that it imposes a special-consent provision, exercisable by a person

other than the woman and her physician, as a prerequisite
to a minor's termination of her pregnancy and does so
without a sufficient justification for the restriction. It violates the strictures of *Roe* and *Doe*.

Saline amniocentesis. Section 9 of the statute prohibits the
use of saline amniocentesis, as a method or technique of
abortion, after the first 12 weeks of pregnancy. It describes the method as one whereby the amniotic fluid is
withdrawn and "a saline or other fluid" is inserted into the
amniotic sac. The statute imposes this proscription on the
ground that the technique "is deleterious to maternal
health," and places it in the form of a legislative finding. . . .

We held in *Roe* that after the first stage, "the state, in promoting its interest in the health of the mother, may, if it
chooses, regulate the abortion procedure in ways that are
reasonably related to maternal health." The question with
respect to Section 9 therefore is whether the flat prohibition of saline amniocentesis is a restriction which
"reasonably relates to the preservation and protection of
maternal health." . . .

The District Court's majority determined, on the basis of
the evidence before it, that the maternal mortality rate in
childbirth does, indeed, exceed the mortality rate where
saline amniocentesis is used. Therefore, the majority acknowledged, Section 9 could be upheld only if there were
safe alternative methods of inducing abortion after the
first 12 weeks. Referring to such methods as hysteroto-
my, hysterectomy, "mechanical means of inducing abortion," and prostaglandin injection, the majority said that at
least the latter two techniques were safer than saline.
Consequently, the majority concluded, the restriction in

Section 9 could be upheld as reasonably related to maternal health.

We feel that the majority, in reaching its conclusion, failed to appreciate and to consider several significant facts. First, it did not recognize the prevalence, as the record conclusively demonstrates, of the use of saline amniocentesis as an accepted medical procedure in this country; the procedure, as noted above, is employed in a substantial majority (the testimony from both sides ranges from 68% to 80%) of all post-first trimester abortions. Second, it failed to recognize that at the time of trial, there were severe limitations on the availability of the prostaglandin technique, which, although promising, was used only on an experimental basis until less than two years before. . . . Third, the statute's reference to the insertion of "a saline or other fluid" appears to include within its proscription the intra-amniotic injection of prostaglandin itself and other methods that may be developed in the future and that may prove highly effective and completely safe. Finally, the majority did not consider the anomaly inherent in Section 9 when it proscribes the use of saline but does not prohibit techniques that are many times more likely to result in maternal death.

These unappreciated or overlooked factors place the State's decision to bar use of the saline method in a completely different light. The State, through Section 9, would prohibit the use of a method which the record shows is the one most commonly used nationally by physicians after the first trimester and which is safer, with respect to maternal mortality, than even continuation of the pregnancy until normal childbirth. Moreover, as a practical matter, it forces a woman and her physician to terminate her pregnancy by methods more dangerous to her health than the method outlawed.

As so viewed, particularly in the light of the present unavailability . . . of the prostaglandin technique, the outright legislative proscription of saline fails as a reasonable regulation for the protection of maternal health. It comes into focus, instead, as an unreasonable or arbitrary regulation designed to inhibit, and having the effect of inhibiting, the vast majority of abortions after the first 12 weeks. As such, it does not withstand constitutional challenge.

Recordkeeping. Sections 10 and 11 of the Act impose recordkeeping requirements for health facilities and physicians concerned with abortions irrespective of the pregnancy stage. Under Section 10, each such facility and physician is to be supplied with forms "the purpose and function of which shall be the preservation of maternal health and life by adding to the sum of medical knowledge through the compilation of relevant maternal health and life data and to monitor all abortions performed to assure that they are done only under and in accordance with the provisions of the law." The statute states that the information on the forms "shall be confidential and shall be used only for statistical purposes." The "records, however, may be inspected and health data acquired by local, state, or national public health officers." Under Section 11 the records are to be kept for seven years in the permanent files of the health facility where the abortion was performed.

. . . . All the judges of the District Court panel, however, viewed these provisions as statistical requirements "essential to the advancement of medical knowledge," and as nothing that would "restrict either the abortion decision itself or the exercise of medical judgment in performing an abortion."

.... Recordkeeping and reporting requirements that are reasonably directed to the preservation of maternal health and that properly respect a patient's confidentiality and privacy are permissible. This surely is so for the period after the first stage of pregnancy, for then the State may enact substantive as well as recordkeeping regulations that are reasonable means of protecting maternal health. As to the first stage, one may argue forcefully ... that the State should not be able to impose any recordkeeping requirements that significantly differ from those imposed with respect to other, and comparable, medical or surgical procedures. We conclude, however, that the provisions of Sections 10 and 11, while perhaps approaching impermissible limits, are not constitutionally offensive in themselves. Recordkeeping of this kind, if not abused or overdone, can be useful to the State's interest in protecting the health of its female citizens, and may be a resource that is relevant to decisions involving medical experience and judgment. The added requirements for confidentiality, with the sole exception for public health officers, and for retention for seven years, a period not unreasonable in length, assist and persuade us in our determination of the constitutional limits. As so regarded, we see no legally significant impact or consequence on the abortion decision or on the physician-patient relationship. We naturally assume, furthermore, that these recordkeeping and record-maintaining provisions will be interpreted and enforced by Missouri's Division of Health in the light of our decision with respect to the Act's other provisions, and that, of course, they will not be utilized in such a way as to accomplish, through the sheer burden of recordkeeping detail, what we have held to be an otherwise unconstitutional restriction. Obviously, the State may not require execution of spousal and parental consent forms that have been invalidated today.

Standard of care. [*Danforth*] appeals from the unanimous decision of the District Court that Section 6(1) of the Act is unconstitutional. That section provides:

> "No person who performs or induces an abortion shall fail to exercise that degree of professional skill, care and diligence to preserve the life and health of the fetus which such person would be required to exercise in order to preserve the life and health of any fetus intended to be born and not aborted. Any physician or person assisting in the abortion who shall fail to take such measures to encourage or to sustain the life of the child, and the death of the child results, shall be deemed guilty of manslaughter. . . . Further, such physician or other person shall be liable in an action for damages."

The District Court held that the first sentence was unconstitutionally overbroad because it failed to exclude from its reach the stage of pregnancy prior to viability.

. . . . We conclude, as did the District Court, that Section 6(1) must stand or fall as a unit. Its provisions are inextricably bound together. And a physician's or other person's criminal failure to protect a liveborn infant surely will be subject to prosecution in Missouri under the State's criminal statutes.

The judgment of the District Court is affirmed [confirmed] in part, and reversed in part, and the case is remanded [sent back to the lower court] for further proceedings consistent with this opinion.

It is so ordered.

JUSTICE STEWART (joined by Justice Powell), concurring: . . . . With respect to the definition of viability in Section 2(2) of the Act, it seems to me that the critical consideration is that the statutory definition has almost no operative significance.   The State has merely required physicians performing abortions to *certify* that the fetus to be aborted is not viable.   While the physician may be punished for failing to issue a certification, he may not be punished for erroneously concluding that the fetus is not viable.   There is thus little chance that a physician's professional decision to perform an abortion will be "chilled."

I agree with the Court that the patient-consent provision in Section 3(2) is constitutional. While Section 3(2) obviously regulates the abortion decision during all stages of pregnancy, including the first trimester, I do not believe it conflicts with the statement in *Roe v. Wade* that "for the period of pregnancy prior to [approximately the end of the first trimester] the attending physician, in consultation with his patient, is free to determine, without regulation by the State, that, in his medical judgment, the patient's pregnancy should be terminated.   If that decision is reached, the judgment may be effectuated by an abortion free of interference by the State."   That statement was made in the context of invalidating a state law aimed at thwarting a woman's decision to have an abortion.   It was not intended to preclude the State from enacting a provision aimed at ensuring that the abortion decision is made in a knowing, intelligent, and voluntary fashion.

.... With respect to the state law's requirement of parental consent, Section 3(4), I think it clear that its primary constitutional deficiency lies in its imposition of an absolute limitation on the minor's right to obtain an abortion. The Court's opinion today in *Belotti v. Baird* suggests that a materially different constitutional issue would be presented under a provision requiring parental consent or consultation in most cases but providing for prompt (i) judicial resolution of any disagreement between the parent and the minor, or (ii) judicial determination that the minor is mature enough to give an informed consent without parental concurrence or that abortion in any event is in the minor's best interest. Such a provision would not impose parental approval as an absolute condition upon the minor's right but would assure in most instances consultation between the parent and child.

There can be little doubt that the State furthers a constitutionally permissible end by encouraging an unmarried pregnant minor to seek the help and advice of her parents in making the very important decision whether or not to bear a child. That is a grave decision, and a girl of tender years, under emotional stress, may be ill-equipped to make it without mature advice and emotional support. It seems unlikely that she will obtain adequate counsel and support from the attending physician at an abortion clinic, where abortions for pregnant minors frequently take place. . . .

JUSTICE WHITE (joined by Chief Justice Burger and Justice Rehnquist), concurring in part and dissenting in part: . . . . [T]he State is not - under Section 3(3) - delegating to the husband the power to vindicate the *State's* interest in the future life of the fetus. It is instead recognizing that the husband has an interest of his own in the life of the fetus which should not be extinguished by the unilateral decision of the wife. It by no means follows, from the fact that the mother's interest in deciding "whether or not to terminate her pregnancy" outweighs the *State's* interest in the potential life of the fetus, that the husband's interest is also outweighed and may not be protected by the state. A father's interest in having a child - perhaps his only child - may be unmatched by any other interest in his life. It is truly surprising that the majority finds in the United States Constitution, as it must in order to justify the result it reaches, a rule that the State must assign a greater value to a mother's decision to cut off a potential human life by abortion than to a father's decision to let it mature into a live child. Such a rule cannot be found there, nor can it be found in *Roe v. Wade.* These are matters which a State should be able to decide free from the suffocating power of the federal judge, purporting to act in the name of the Constitution.

In describing the nature of a mother's interest in terminating a pregnancy, the Court in *Roe v. Wade* mentioned only the post-birth burdens of rearing a child and rejected a rule based on her interest in controlling her own body during pregnancy. Missouri has a law which prevents a woman from putting a child up for adoption over her husband's objection. This law represents a judgment by the State that the mother's interest in avoiding the burdens of child rearing do not outweigh or snuff out the father's interest in participating in bringing up his own child. That law is plainly valid, but no more so than Section 3(3) of the Act now before us, resting as it does on precisely the same judgment.

.... Missouri is entitled to protect the minor unmarried woman from making the decision in a way which is not in her own best interests, and it seeks to achieve this goal by requiring parental consultation and consent. This is the traditional way by which States have sought to protect children from their own immature and improvident decisions; and there is absolutely no reason expressed by the majority why the State may not utilize that method here.

Section 9 of the Act prohibits abortion by the method known as saline amniocentesis - a method used at the time the Act was passed for 70% of abortions performed after the first trimester. Legislative history reveals that the Missouri Legislature viewed saline amniocentesis as far less safe a method of abortion than the so-called prostaglandin method. . . .

The District Court . . . cited considerable evidence establishing that the prostaglandin method is safer. In fact, the Chief of Obstetrics at Yale University, Dr. Anderson, suggested that "physicians should be liable for malpractice if they chose saline over prostaglandin after having been given all the facts on both methods." The Court nevertheless reverses the decision of the District Court sustaining [approving] Section 9 against constitutional challenge. It does so apparently because saline amniocentesis was widely used before the Act was passed; because the prostaglandin method was seldom used and was not generally available; and because other abortion techniques more dangerous than saline amniocentesis were not banned. At bottom the majority's holding . . . rests on its *factual* finding that the prostaglandin method is unavailable to the women of Missouri. It therefore concludes that the ban on the saline method is "an unreasonable or arbitrary regulation designed to inhibit, and having the effect of inhibiting, the vast majority of abortions after the first 12 weeks." . . .

Absent proof of a fact essential to its unconstitutionality, the statute remains in effect.

. . . . In any event, the point of Section 9 is to change the practice under which most abortions were performed under the saline amniocentesis method and to make the safer prostaglandin method generally available. It promises to achieve that result, if it remains operative, and the evidence discloses that the result is a desirable one or at least that the legislature could have so viewed it. That should end our inquiry, unless we purport to be not only the country's continuous constitutional convention but also its ex officio medical board with powers to approve or disapprove medical and operative practices and standards throughout the United States.

Section 6(1) of the Act provides:

"No person who performs or induces an abortion shall fail to exercise that degree of professional skill, care and diligence to preserve the life and health of the fetus which such person would be required to exercise in order to preserve the life and health of any fetus intended to be born and not aborted. Any physician or person assisting in the abortion who shall fail to take such measures to encourage or to sustain the life of the child, and the death of the child results, shall be deemed guilty of manslaughter. . . . Further, such physician or other person shall be liable in an action for damages."

If this section is read in any way other than through a microscope, it is plainly intended to require that, where a "fetus [may have] the capability of meaningful life outside the mother's womb," the abortion be handled in a way which is designed to preserve that life notwithstanding the mother's desire to terminate it. Indeed, even looked at through a microscope the statute seems to go no further. It requires a physician to exercise "*that* degree of professional skill . . . to preserve the . . . fetus," which he would be required to exercise if the mother wanted a live child. Plainly, if the pregnancy is to be terminated at a time when there is no chance of life outside the womb, a physician would not be required to exercise any care or skill to preserve the life of the fetus during abortion no matter what the mother's desires. The statute would appear then to operate only in the gray area after the fetus *might* be viable but while the physician is still able to certify "with reasonable medical certainty that the fetus is not viable." . . . Since the State has a compelling interest, sufficient to outweigh the mother's desire to kill the fetus, when the "fetus . . . has the capability of meaningful life outside the mother's womb," the statute is constitutional.

Incredibly, the Court reads the statute instead to require "the physician to preserve the life and health of the fetus, whatever the stage of pregnancy," thereby attributing to the Missouri Legislature the strange intention of passing a statute with absolutely no chance of surviving constitutional challenge under *Roe v. Wade.*

The Court compounds its error by also striking down as unseverable the wholly unobjectionable requirement in the second sentence of Section 6(1) that where an abortion produces a live child, steps must be taken to sustain its life. It explains its result in two sentences:

"We conclude, as did the District Court, that Section 6(1) must stand or fall as a unit. Its provisions are inextricably bound together."

The question whether a constitutional provision of state law is severable from an unconstitutional provision is *entirely* a question of the intent of the state legislature. There is not the slightest reason to suppose that the Missouri Legislature would not require proper care for live babies just because it cannot require physicians performing abortions to take care to preserve the life of fetuses. The Attorney General of Missouri has argued here that the *only* intent of Section 6(1) was to require physicians to support a live baby which resulted from an abortion.

At worst, Section 6(1) is ambiguous on both points and the District Court should be directed to abstain until a construction may be had from the state courts. Under no circumstances should Section 6(1) be declared unconstitutional at this point. . . .

JUSTICE STEVENS, concurring in part and dissenting in part: . . . . In *Roe v. Wade*, the Court held that a woman's right to decide whether to abort a pregnancy is entitled to constitutional protection. . . .

If two abortion procedures had been equally accessible to Missouri women, in my judgment the United States Constitution would not prevent the state legislature from outlawing the one it found to be the less safe even though its conclusion might not reflect a unanimous consensus of informed medical opinion. However, the record indicates that when the Missouri statute was enacted, a prohibition of the saline amniocentesis procedure was almost tantamount to a prohibition of any abortion in the State after the first 12 weeks of pregnancy. Such a prohibition is inconsistent with the essential holding of *Roe v. Wade* and therefore cannot stand.

In my opinion, however, the parental-consent requirement is consistent with the holding in *Roe.* The State's interest in the welfare of its young citizens justifies a variety of protective measures. Because he may not foresee the consequences of his decision, a minor may not make an enforceable bargain. He may not lawfully work or travel where he pleases, or even attend exhibitions of constitutionally protected adult motion pictures. Persons below a certain age may not marry without parental consent. Indeed, such consent is essential even when the young woman is already pregnant. The State's interest in protecting a young person from harm justifies the imposition of restraints on his or her freedom even though comparable restraints on adults would be constitutionally impermissible. Therefore, the holding in *Roe v. Wade* that the abortion decision is entitled to constitutional protection merely emphasizes the importance of the decision; it does not lead to the conclusion that the state legislature has no power to enact legislation for the purpose of protecting a young pregnant woman from the consequences of an incorrect decision.

The abortion decision is, of course, more important than the decision to attend or to avoid an adult motion picture, or the decision to work long hours in factory. It is not necessarily any more important than the decision to run away from home or the decision to marry. But even if it is the most important kind of a decision a young person may ever make, that assumption merely enhances the quality of the State's interest in maximizing the probability that the decision be made correctly and with full understanding of the consequences of either alternative.

The Court recognizes that the State may insist that the decision not be made without the benefit of medical advice. But since the most significant consequences of the decision are not medical in character, it would seem to me that the State may, with equal legitimacy, insist that the decision be made only after other appropriate counsel has been had as well. Whatever choice a pregnant young woman makes - to marry, to abort, to bear her child out of wedlock - the consequences of her decision may have a profound impact on her entire future life. A legislative determination that such a choice will be made more wisely in most cases if the advice and moral support of a parent play a part in the decisionmaking process is surely not irrational. Moreover, it is perfectly clear that the parental-consent requirement will necessarily involve a parent in the decisional process.

If there is no parental-consent requirement, many minors will submit to the abortion procedure without ever informing their parents. An assumption that the parental reaction will be hostile, disparaging, or violent no doubt persuades many children simply to bypass parental counsel which would in fact be loving, supportive, and, indeed, for some indispensable. It is unrealistic, in my judgment, to assume that every parent-child relationship is either (a) so perfect that communication and accord will take place routinely or (b) so imperfect that the absence of communication reflects the child's correct prediction that the parent will exercise his or her veto arbitrarily to further a selfish interest rather than the child's interest. A state legislature may conclude that most parents will be primarily interested in the welfare of their children, and fur-

ther, that the imposition of a parental-consent requirement is an appropriate method of giving the parents an
opportunity to foster that welfare by helping a pregnant
distressed child to make and to implement a correct decision.

The State's interest is not dependent on an estimate of the
impact the parental-consent requirement may have on the
total number of abortions that may take place. I assume
that parents will sometimes prevent abortions which
might better be performed; other parents may advise
abortions that should not be performed. Similarly, even
doctors are not omniscient; specialists in performing abortions may incorrectly conclude that the immediate advan-
tages of the procedure outweigh the disadvantages which
a parent could evaluate in better perspective. In each individual case factors much more profound than a mere
medical judgment may weigh heavily in the scales. The
overriding consideration is that the right to make the
choice be exercised as wisely as possible.

The Court assumes that parental consent is an appropriate
requirement if the minor is not capable of understanding
the procedure and of appreciating its consequences and
those of available alternatives. This assumption is, of
course, correct and consistent with the predicate which
underlies all state legislation seeking to protect minors
from the consequences of decisions they are not yet prepared to make. In all such situations chronological age
has been the basis for imposition of a restraint on the
minor's freedom of choice even though it is perfectly obvious that such a yardstick is imprecise and perhaps even
unjust in particular cases. The Court seems to assume that
the capacity to conceive a child and the judgment of the
physician are the only constitutionally permissible yard-

sticks for determining whether a young woman can independently make the abortion decision. I doubt the accuracy of the Court's empirical judgment. Even if it were correct, however, as a matter of constitutional law I think a State has power to conclude otherwise and to select a chronological age as its standard.

In short, the State's interest in the welfare of its young citizens is sufficient, in my judgment, to support the parental-consent requirement.

BEAL v. DOE

EXCERPTS

"*Roe* did not declare an unqualified 'constitutional right to an abortion.' . . . Rather, the right protects the woman from unduly burdensome interference with her freedom to decide whether to terminate her pregnancy. It implies no limitation on the authority of a State to make a value judgment favoring childbirth over abortion, and to implement that judgment by the allocation of public funds."

Justice Lewis Powell

"At viability, usually in the third trimester, the State's interest in the potential life of the fetus justifies prohibition with criminal penalties, except where the life or the health of the mother is threatened."

Justice Lewis Powell

"The stark reality for too many, not just 'some,' indigent pregnant women is that indigency makes access to competent licenses physicians not merely 'difficult' but 'impossible.'"

Justice William Brennan

In Brief

Question: Should Medicaid pay for elective abortions?

Lower Court: U.S. District Court, Western Pennsylvania
U.S. Court of Appeals, Third Circuit

Law: Title XIX of the Social Security Act (Medicaid)

Parties: Frank S. Beal, Secretary, Pennsylvania
Department of Public Welfare
Ann Doe, pseudonym of an indigent

Counsel: For Beal: Norman J. Watkins
For Doe: Judd F. Crosby

Arguments: January 11, 1977

Decision: June 20, 1977

Majority: Chief Justice Burger, Justices Stewart, White,
Powell, Rehnquist, Stevens

Minority: Justices Brennan, Marshall, Blackmun

Decision by: Justice Powell (p. 109)

Dissents: Justice Brennan (p. 112)
Justice Marshall (p. 114)
Justice Blackmun (p. 117)

Offical Text: U.S. Reports, Vol. 432, p. 438

Lower Court: Federal Supplement, Vol. 376, p. 173
Federal Reporter 2nd, Vol. 523, p. 611

THE BEAL COURT

Chief Justice Warren Burger
Appointed 1969 by Richard M. Nixon

Associate Justice William Brennan
Appointed 1956 by Dwight D. Eisenhower

Associate Justice Potter Stewart
Appointed 1958 by Dwight D. Eisenhower

Associate Justice Byron White
Appointed 1962 by John F. Kennedy

Associate Justice Thurgood Marshall
Appointed 1967 by Lyndon B. Johnson

Associate Justice Harry Blackmun
Appointed 1970 by Richard M. Nixon

Associate Justice Lewis Powell
Appointed 1972 by Richard M. Nixon

Associate Justice William Rehnquist
Appointed 1971 by Richard M. Nixon

Associate Justice John Paul Stevens
Appointed 1975 by Gerald R. Ford

BEAL v. DOE

June 20, 1977

JUSTICE POWELL: The issue in this case is whether Title XIX of the Social Security Act . . . requires States that participate in the Medical Assistance (Medicaid) program to fund the cost of nontherapeutic abortions.

Title XIX establishes the Medicaid program under which participating States may provide federally funded medical assistance to needy persons. The statute requires participating States to provide qualified individuals with financial assistance in five general categories of medical treatment. Although Title XIX does not require States to provide funding for all medical treatment falling within the five general categories, it does require that state Medicaid plans establish "reasonable standards . . . for determining . . . the extent of medical assistance under the plan . . . consistent with the objectives of [Title XIX]."

[Doe], who [is] eligible for medical assistance under Pennsylvania's federally approved Medicaid plan, [was] denied financial assistance for desired abortions pursuant to Pennsylvania regulations limiting such assistance to those abortions that are certified by physicians as medically necessary. When [Doe's application] for Medicaid assistance [was] denied because of [her] failure to furnish the required certificates, [she] filed this action in United States District Court for the Western District of Pennsylvania . . . alleg[ing] that Pennsylvania's requirement of a certificate of medical necessity contravened relevant provisions of Title XIX and denied [her] equal protection of the laws in violation of the Fourteenth Amendment.

. . . . [T]he court [held] that the Pennsylvania requirement was unconstitutional as applied during the first
trimester. The United States Court of Appeals for the
Third Circuit . . . [held] that Title XIX prohibits participating States from requiring a physician's certificate of
medical necessity as a condition for funding during both
the first and second trimesters of pregnancy. . . .

We granted certiorari [agreed to hear the case] to resolve
a conflict among the federal courts as to the requirements
of Title XIX.

The only question before us is . . . whether Title XIX requires Pennsylvania to fund under its Medicaid program
the cost of *all* abortions that are permissible under state
law. "The starting point in every case involving construction of a statute is the language itself." Title XIX makes
no reference to abortions, or, for that matter, to any other
particular medical procedure. Instead, the statute is cast
in terms that require participating States to provide financial assistance with respect to five broad categories of
medical treatment. But nothing in the statute suggests
that participating States are required to fund every medical procedure that falls within the delineated categories of
medical care. . . .

Pennsylvania's regulation comports fully with Title XIX's
broadly stated primary objective to enable each State, as
far as practicable, to furnish medical assistance to individuals whose income and resources are insufficient to meet
the costs of necessary medical services. Although serious
statutory questions might be presented if a state Medicaid
plan excluded necessary medical treatment from its coverage, it is hardly inconsistent with the objectives of the Act

for a State to refuse to fund *unnecessary* - though perhaps desirable - medical services.

. . . . Our interpretation of the statute is reinforced by two other relevant considerations. First, when Congress passed Title XIX in 1965, nontherapeutic abortions were unlawful in most States. In view of the then-prevailing state law, the contention that Congress intended to require - rather than permit - participating States to fund nontherapeutic abortions requires far more convincing proof than . . . offered. Second, the Department of Health, Education, and Welfare, the agency charged with the administration of this complicated statute, takes the position that Title XIX allows - but does not mandate - funding for such abortions. "[W]e must be mindful that 'the construction of a statute by those charged with its execution should be followed unless there are compelling indications that it is wrong. . . .'" Here, such indications are completely absent.

We therefore hold that Pennsylvania's refusal to extend Medicaid coverage to nontherapeutic abortions is not inconsistent with Title XIX. We make clear, however, that the federal statute leaves a State free to provide such coverage if it so desires.

There is one feature of the Pennsylvania Medicaid program, not addressed by the Court of Appeals, that may conflict with Title XIX. Under the Pennsylvania program, financial assistance is not provided for medically necessary abortions unless two physicians in addition to the attending physician have examined the patient and have concurred in writing that the abortion is medically necessary. On this record, we are unable to determine the precise role played by these two additional physicians, and consequently we are unable to ascertain whether this requirement interferes with the attending physician's medical judgment in a manner not contemplated by the Congress. The judgment of the Court of Appeals is therefore reversed, and the case is remanded [returned to the lower court] for consideration of this requirement.

It is so ordered.

JUSTICE BRENNAN (joined by Justices Marshall and Blackmun), dissenting: The Court holds that the "necessary medical services" which Pennsylvania must fund for individuals eligible for Medicaid do not include services connected with elective abortions. I dissent.

. . . . Pregnancy is unquestionably a condition requiring medical services. Treatment for the condition may involve medical procedures for its termination, or medical procedures to bring the pregnancy to term, resulting in a live birth. "[A]bortion and childbirth, when stripped of the sensitive moral arguments surrounding the abortion controversy, are simply two alternative medical methods of dealing with pregnancy. . . ." The Medicaid statutes leave the decision as to choice among pregnancy procedures exclusively with the doctor and his patient, and make no provision whatever for intervention by the State in that decision. Section 1396a(a)(19) expressly imposes the obligation upon participating States to incorporate safeguards in their programs that assure medical "care and services will be provided, in a manner consistent with . . . the best interests of the recipients." And, significantly, the Senate Finance Committee Report on the Medicaid bill expressly stated that the "physician is to be the key figure in determining utilization of health services." Thus the very heart of the congressional scheme is that the physician and patient should have complete freedom to choose those medical procedures for a given condition which are best suited to the needs of the patient.

The Court's original abortion decisions dovetail precisely with the congressional purpose under Medicaid to avoid interference with the decision of the woman and her physician. *Roe v. Wade* held that "[t]he attending physician, in consultation with his patient, is free to determine, without regulation by the State, that, in his medical judgment, the patient's pregnancy should be terminated." And *Doe v. Bolton* held that "the medical judgment may be exercised in the light of all factors - physical, emotional, psychological, familial, and the woman's age - relevant to the well-being of the patient. All these factors may relate to health. This allows the attending physician the room he needs to make his best medical judgment. And it is room that operates for the benefit, not the disadvantage, of the pregnant woman." Once medical treatment of some sort is necessary, Title XIX does not dictate what that treatment should be. In the face of Title XIX's emphasis upon the joint autonomy of the physician and his patient in the decision of how to treat the condition of pregnancy, it is beyond comprehension how treatment for therapeutic abortions and live births constitutes "necessary medical services" under Title XIX, but that for elective abortions does not.

. . . . It is no answer that abortions were illegal in 1965 when Medicaid was enacted, and in 1972 when the family-planning amendment was adopted. Medicaid deals with general categories of medical services, not with specific procedures, and nothing in the statute even suggests that Medicaid is designed to assist in payment for only those medical services that were legally permissible in 1965 and 1972. . . .

[T]here is certainly no affirmative policy justification of the State that aids the Court's construction of "necessary medical services" as not including medical services rendered in performing elective abortions. The State cannot contend that it protects its fiscal interests in not funding elective abortions when it incurs far greater expense in paying for the more costly medical services performed in carrying pregnancies to term, and, after birth, paying the increased welfare bill incurred to support the mother and child. Nor can the State contend that it protects the mother's health by discouraging an abortion, for not only may Pennsylvania's exclusion force the pregnant woman to use of measures dangerous to her life and health but, as *Roe v. Wade* concluded, elective abortions by competent licensed physicians are now "relatively safe" and the risks to women undergoing abortions by such means "appear to be as low as or lower than . . . for normal childbirth."

The Court's construction can only result as a practical matter in forcing penniless pregnant women to have children they would not have borne if the State had not weighted the scales to make their choice to have abortions substantially more onerous. . . .

I would affirm the judgment of the Court of Appeals.

JUSTICE MARSHALL, dissenting (This opinion also applies to *Maher v. Roe* and *Poelker v. Doe*]: . . . It is all too obvious that the governmental actions in these cases, ostensibly taken to "encourage" women to carry pregnancies to term, are in reality intended to impose a moral viewpoint that no State may constitutionally enforce. Since efforts to overturn those decisions [*Roe* and *Doe*] have been unsuccessful, the opponents of abortion have attempted every imaginable means to circumvent the commands of the Constitution and impose their moral choices upon the rest of society. The present cases involve the most vicious attacks yet devised. The impact of the regulations here falls tragically upon those among us least able to help or defend themselves. As the Court well knows, these regulations inevitably will have the practical effect of preventing nearly all poor women from obtaining safe and legal abortions.

. . . . The governmental benefits at issue here, while perhaps not representing large amounts of money for any individual, are nevertheless of absolutely vital importance in the lives of the recipients. The right of every woman to choose whether to bear a child is, as *Roe v. Wade* held, of fundamental importance. An unwanted child may be disruptive and destructive of the life of any woman, but the impact is felt most by those too poor to ameliorate those effects. If funds for an abortion are unavailable, a poor woman may feel that she is forced to obtain an illegal abortion that poses a serious threat to her health and even her life. If she refuses to take this risk, and undergoes the pain and danger of state-financed pregnancy and childbirth, she may well give up all chance of escaping the cycle of poverty. Absent day-care facilities, she will be forced into full-time child care for years to come; she will be unable to work so that her family can break out of the welfare system or the lowest income brackets. If she already has children, another infant to feed and clothe may well stretch the budget past the breaking point. All chance to control the direction of her own life will have been lost.

.... While poverty alone does not entitle a class to claim government benefits, it is surely a relevant factor in the present inquiry. . . . Medicaid recipients are, almost by definition, "completely unable to pay for" abortions, and are thereby completely denied "a meaningful opportunity" to obtain them.

It is no less disturbing that the effect of the challenged regulations will fall with great disparity upon women of minority races. Nonwhite women now obtain abortions at nearly twice the rate of whites, and it appears that almost 40 percent of minority women - more than five times the proportion of whites - are dependent upon Medicaid for their health care. Even if this strongly disparate racial impact does not alone violate the Equal Protection Clause, "at some point a showing that state action has a devastating impact on the lives of minority racial groups must be relevant."

Against the brutal effect that the challenged laws will have must be weighed the asserted state interest. The Court describes this as a "strong interest in protecting the potential life of the fetus." Yet in *Doe v. Bolton* the Court expressly held that any state interest during the first trimester of pregnancy, when 86 percent of all abortions occur, was wholly insufficient to justify state interference with the right to abortion. If a State's interest in potential human life before the point of viability is insufficient to justify requiring several physicians' concurrence for an abortion, I cannot comprehend how it magically becomes adequate to allow the present infringement on rights of disfavored classes. If there is any state interest in potential life before the point of viability, it certainly does not outweigh the deprivation or serious discouragement of a vital constitutional right of especial importance to poor and minority women.

Thus, taking account of all relevant factors under the flexible standard of equal protection review, I would hold the Connecticut and Pennsylvania Medicaid regulations and the St. Louis public hospital policy violative of the Fourteenth Amendment.

When this Court decided *Roe v. Wade* and *Doe v. Bolton*, it properly embarked on a course of constitutional adjudication no less controversial than that begun by *Brown v. Board of Education*. The abortion decisions are sound law and undoubtedly good policy. They have never been questioned by the Court and we are told that today's cases "signa[l] no retreat from *Roe* or the cases applying it." The logic of those cases inexorably requires invalidation of the present enactments. Yet I fear that the Court's decisions will be an invitation to public officials, already under extraordinary pressure from well-financed and carefully orchestrated lobbying campaigns, to approve more such restrictions. The effect will be to relegate millions of people to lives of poverty and despair. When elected leaders cower before public pressure, this Court, more than ever, must not shirk its duty to enforce the Constitution for the benefit of the poor and powerless.

JUSTICE BLACKMUN (joined by Justices Brennan and Marshall), dissenting [This opinion also applies to *Maher v. Roe* and *Poelker v. Doe*]: The Court today, by its decisions in these cases, allows the States, and such municipalities as choose to do so, to accomplish indirectly what the Court in *Roe v. Wade* and *Doe v. Bolton* - by a substantial majority and with some emphasis, I had thought - said they could not do directly. The Court concedes the existence of a constitutional right but denies the realization and enjoyment of that right on the ground that existence and realization are separate and distinct. For the individual woman concerned, indigent and financially helpless, as the Court's opinions in the three cases concede her to be, the result is punitive and tragic. Implicit in the Court's holdings is the condescension that she may go elsewhere for her abortion. I find that disingenuous and alarming, almost reminiscent of: "Let them eat cake."

The result the Court reaches is particularly distressing in *Poelker v. Doe*, where a presumed majority, in electing as mayor one whom the record shows campaigned on the issue of closing public hospitals to nontherapeutic abortions, punitively impresses upon a needy minority its own concepts of the socially desirable, the publicly acceptable, and the morally sound, with a touch of the devil-take-the-hindmost. This is not the kind of thing for which our Constitution stands.

The Court's financial argument, of course, is specious. To be sure, welfare funds are limited and welfare must be spread perhaps as best meets the community's concept of its needs. But the cost of a nontherapeutic abortion is far less than the cost of maternity care and delivery, and holds no comparison whatsoever with the welfare costs that will burden the State for the new indigents and their support in the long, long years ahead.

Neither is it an acceptable answer, as the Court well knows, to say that the Congress and the States are free to authorize the use of funds for nontherapeutic abortions. Why should any politician incur the demonstrated wrath and noise of the abortion opponents when mere silence and nonactivity accomplish the results the opponents want?

There is another world "out there," the existence of which the Court, I suspect, either chooses to ignore or fears to recognize. And so the cancer of poverty will continue to grow. This is a sad day for those who regard the Constitution as a force that would serve justice to all evenhandedly and, in so doing, would better the lot of the poorest among us.

MAHER v. ROE

EXCERPTS

"The Court's construction can only result as a practical matter in forcing penniless pregnant women to have children they would not have borne if the State had not weighted the scales to make their choice to have abortions substantially more onerous. . ."

Justice William Brennan

"There is another world 'out there,' the existence of which the Court, I suspect, either chooses to ignore or fears to recognize. And so the cancer of poverty will continue to grow. This is a sad day for those who regard the Constitution as a force that would serve justice to all evenhandedly and, in so doing, would better the lot of the poorest among us."

Justice Harry Blackmun

In Brief

Question: Should Medicaid pay for elective abortions?

Lower Court: U.S. District Court, Connecticut
                U.S. Court of Appeals, Second Circuit

Law: Title XIX of the Social Security Act (Medicaid)

Parties: Edward Maher, Connecticut Commissioner
                 of Social Services
                Susan Roe, pseudonyn of an indigent

Counsel: For Maher: Edmund Walsh
                For Roe: Lucy Katz

Arguments: January 11, 1977

Decision: June 20, 1977

Majority: Chief Justice Burger, Justices Stewart, White,
                Powell, Rehnquist, Stevens

Minority: Justices Brennan, Marshall, Blackmun

Decision by: Justice Powell (p. 125)

Concurrence: Chief Justice Burger (p. 130)

Dissents: Justice Brennan (p. 131)
                Justice Marshall (see *Beal*, p. 114)
                Justice Blackmun (see *Beal*, p. 117)

Offical Text: U.S. Reports, Vol. 432, p. 464
Lower Court: Federal Supplement, Vol. 380, p. 726
                Federal Reporter 2nd, Vol. 522, p. 928

THE MAHER COURT

Chief Justice Warren Burger
Appointed 1969 by Richard M. Nixon

Associate Justice William Brennan
Appointed 1956 by Dwight D. Eiscnhower

Associate Justice Potter Stewart
Appointed 1958 by Dwight D. Eisenhower

Associate Justice Byron White
Appointed 1962 by John F. Kennedy

Associate Justice Thurgood Marshall
Appointed 1967 by Lyndon B. Johnson

Associate Justice Harry Blackmun
Appointed 1970 by Richard M. Nixon

Associate Justice Lewis Powell
Appointed 1972 by Richard M. Nixon

Associate Justice William Rehnquist
Appointed 1971 by Richard M. Nixon

Associate Justice John Paul Stevens
Appointed 1975 by Gerald R. Ford

MAHER v. ROE

June 20, 1977

JUSTICE POWELL: .... In this case ... we must decide whether the Constitution requires a participating State [in the Medicaid program] to pay for nontherapeutic abortions when it pays for childbirth.

A regulation of the Connecticut Welfare Department limits state Medicaid benefits for first trimester abortions to those that are "medically necessary." ... In order to obtain authorization for a first trimester abortion, the hospital or clinic where the abortion is to be performed must submit, among other things, a certificate from the patient's attending physician stating that the abortion is medically necessary.

This attack on the validity of the Connecticut regulation was brought against appellant Maher, the Commissioner of Social Services, by appellees Poe and Roe, the indigent women who were unable to obtain a physician's certificate of medical necessity. ... [T]hey challenged the regulation both as inconsistent with the requirements of Title XIX of the Social Security Act, and as violative of their constitutional rights, including the Fourteenth Amendment's guarantees of due process and equal protection. ...

The Constitution imposes no obligation on the States to pay the pregnancy-related medical expenses of indigent women, or indeed to pay any of the medical expenses of indigents. But when a State decides to alleviate some of the hardships of poverty by providing medical care, the manner in which it dispenses benefits is subject to constitutional limitations.   [Roe's] claim is that Connecticut must accord equal treatment to both abortion and childbirth, and may not evidence a policy preference by funding only the medical expenses incident to childbirth. This challenge to the classifications established by the Connecticut regulation presents a question arising under the Equal Protection Clause of the Fourteenth Amendment. . . .

[W]e think the District Court erred in holding that the Connecticut regulation violated the Equal Protection Clause of the Fourteenth Amendment.

. . . . In a sense, every denial of welfare to an indigent creates a wealth classification as compared to nonindigents who are able to pay for the desired goods or services. But . . . the central question in this case is whether the regulation "impinges upon a fundamental right explicitly or implicitly protected by the Constitution." The District Court read our decisions in *Roe v. Wade*, and the subsequent cases applying it, as establishing a fundamental right to abortion and therefore concluded that nothing less than a compelling state interest would justify Connecticut's different treatment of abortion and childbirth. We think the District Court misconceived the nature and scope of the fundamental right recognized in *Roe*.

At issue in *Roe* was the constitutionality of a Texas law making it a crime to procure or attempt to procure an abortion, except on medical advice for the purpose of saving the life of the mother. Drawing on a group of disparate cases restricting governmental intrusion, physical coercion, and criminal prohibition of certain activities, we concluded that the Fourteenth Amendment's concept of personal liberty affords constitutional protection against state interference with certain aspects of an individual's personal "privacy," including a woman's decision to terminate her pregnancy.

The Texas statute imposed severe criminal sanctions on the physicians and other medical personnel who performed abortions, thus drastically limiting the availability and safety of the desired service. . . . We held that only a compelling state interest would justify such a sweeping restriction on a constitutionally protected interest, and we found no such state interest during the first trimester. Even when judged against this demanding standard, however, the State's dual interest in the health of the pregnant woman and the potential life of the fetus were deemed sufficient to justify substantial regulation of abortions in the second and third trimesters. "These interests are separate and distinct. Each grows in substantiality as the woman approaches term and, at a point during pregnancy, each becomes 'compelling.'" In the second trimester, the State's interest in the health of the pregnant woman justifies state regulation reasonably related to that concern. At viability, usually in the third trimester, the State's interest in the potential life of the fetus justifies prohibition with criminal penalties, except where the life or health of the mother is threatened.

The Texas law in *Roe* was a stark example of impermissible interference with the pregnant woman's decision to terminate her pregnancy. In subsequent cases, we have invalidated other types of restrictions, different in form but similar in effect, on the woman's freedom of choice. Thus, in *Planned Parenthood of Central Missouri v. Danforth*, we held that Missouri's requirement of spousal consent was unconstitutional because it "granted [the husband] the right to prevent unilaterally, and for whatever reason, the effectuation of his wife's and her physician's decision to terminate her pregnancy." . . . Although a state-created obstacle need not be absolute to be impermissible, we have held that a requirement for a lawful abortion "is not unconstitutional unless it unduly burdens the right to seek an abortion." . . .

Roe did not declare an unqualified "constitutional right to an abortion," as the District Court seemed to think. Rather, the right protects the woman from unduly burdensome interference with her freedom to decide whether to terminate her pregnancy. It implies no limitation on the authority of a State to make a value judgment favoring childbirth over abortion, and to implement that judgment by the allocation of public funds.

The Connecticut regulation before us is different in kind from the laws invalidated in our previous abortion decisions. The Connecticut regulation places no obstacles - absolute or otherwise - in the pregnant woman's path to an abortion. An indigent woman who desires an abortion suffers no disadvantage as a consequence of Connecticut's decision to fund childbirth; she continues as before to be dependent on private sources for the service she desires. The State may have made childbirth a more attractive alternative, thereby influencing the woman's decision, but it has imposed no restriction on access to abortions that was not already there. The indigency that may make it difficult - and in some cases, perhaps, impossible - for some women to have abortions is neither created nor in any way affected by the Connecticut regulation. We conclude that the Connecticut regulation does not impinge upon the fundamental right recognized in *Roe.*

.... *Roe* itself explicitly acknowledged the State's strong interest in protecting the potential life of the fetus. That interest exists throughout the pregnancy, "grow[ing] in substantiality as the woman approaches term." Because the pregnant woman carries a potential human being, she "cannot be isolated in her privacy. ... [Her] privacy is no longer sole and any right of privacy she possesses must be measured accordingly." The State unquestionably has a "strong and legitimate interest in encouraging normal childbirth," an interest honored over the centuries. Nor can there be any question that the Connecticut regulation rationally furthers that interest. The medical costs associated with childbirth are substantial, and have increased significantly in recent years. As recognized by the District Court in this case, such costs are significantly greater than those normally associated with elective abortions during the first trimester. The subsidizing of costs incident to childbirth is a rational means of encouraging childbirth.

We certainly are not unsympathetic to the plight of an indigent woman who desires an abortion, but "the Constitution does not provide judicial remedies for every social and economic ill." ...

The decision whether to expend state funds for nontherapeutic abortion is fraught with judgments of policy and value over which opinions are sharply divided. Our conclusion that the Connecticut regulation is constitutional is not based on a weighing of its wisdom or social desirability, for this Court does not strike down state laws "because they may be unwise, improvident, or out of harmony with a particular school of thought." Indeed, when an issue involves policy choices as sensitive as those implicated by public funding of nontherapeutic abortions, the appropri-

ate forum for their resolution in a democracy is the legislature. We should not forget that "legislatures are ulti-
mate guardians of the liberties and welfare of the people
in quite as great a degree as the courts."

In conclusion, we emphasize that our decision today does
not proscribe government funding of nontherapeutic
abortions. It is open to Congress to require provision of
Medicaid benefits for such abortions as a condition of
state participation in the Medicaid program. Also, under
Title XIX as construed in *Beal v. Doe*, Connecticut is free
- through normal democratic processes - to decide that
such benefits should be provided. We hold only that the
Constitution does not require a judicially imposed resolution of these difficult issues.

The District Court also invalidated Connecticut's requirements of prior written consent by the pregnant woman
and prior authorization by the Department of Social Services. . . . It is not unreasonable for a State to insist upon a
prior showing of medical necessity to insure that its money is being spent only for authorized purposes. . . . In
Planned Parenthood of Central Missouri v. Danforth, we
held that the woman's written consent to an abortion was
not an impermissible burden under *Roe*. We think that
decision is controlling on the similar issue here.

The judgment of the District Court is reversed, and the
case is remanded [returned to the lower court] for further
proceedings consistent with this opinion.

It is so ordered.

CHIEF JUSTICE BURGER, concurring: I join the Court's
opinion. Like the Court, I do not read any decision of this

Court as requiring a State to finance a nontherapeutic abortion. The Court's holdings in *Roe v. Wade* and *Doe v. Bolton* simply require that a State not create an absolute barrier to a woman's decision to have an abortion. These precedents do not suggest that the State is constitutionally required to assist her in procuring it.

From time to time, every state legislature determines that, as a matter of sound public policy, the government ought to provide certain health and social services to its citizens. Encouragement of childbirth and child care is not a novel undertaking in this regard. Various governments, both in this country and in others, have made such a determination for centuries. In recent times, they have similarly provided educational services. The decision to provide any one of these services - or not to provide them - is not required by the Federal Constitution. Nor does the providing of a particular service require, as a matter of federal constitutional law, the provision of another.

Here, the State of Connecticut has determined that it will finance certain childbirth expenses. That legislative determination places no state-created barrier to a woman's choice to procure an abortion, and it does not require the State to provide it. Accordingly, I concur in the judgment.

JUSTICE BRENNAN (joined by Justices Marshall and Blackmun), dissenting: . . . . The stark reality for too many, not just "some," indigent pregnant women is that indigency makes access to competent licensed physicians not merely "difficult" but "impossible." As a practical matter, many indigent women will feel they have no choice but to carry their pregnancies to term because the State will pay for the associated medical services, even

though they would have chosen to have abortions if the
State had also provided funds for that procedure, or indeed if the State had provided funds for neither procedure. This disparity in funding by the State clearly operates to coerce indigent pregnant women to bear children
they would not otherwise choose to have, and just as clearly, this coercion can only operate upon the poor, who
are uniquely the victims of this form of financial pressure. . . .

None can take seriously the Court's assurance that its
"conclusion signals no retreat from *Roe [v. Wade]* or the
cases applying it." That statement must occasion great
surprise among the Courts of Appeals and District Courts
that, relying upon *Roe v. Wade* and *Doe v. Bolton*, have
held that States are constitutionally required to fund
elective abortions if they fund pregnancies carried to
term. . . .

Roe v. Wade and cases following it hold that an area of
privacy invulnerable to the State's intrusion surrounds the
decision of a pregnant woman whether or not to carry her
pregnancy to term. The Connecticut scheme clearly infringes upon that area of privacy by bringing financial
pressures on indigent women that force them to bear children they would not otherwise have. That is an obvious
impairment of the fundamental right established by *Roe
v. Wade.* Yet the Court concludes that "the Connecticut
regulation does not impinge upon [that] fundamental
right." This conclusion is based on a perceived distinction,
on the one hand, between the imposition of criminal penalties for the procurement of an abortion present in *Roe
v. Wade* and *Doe v. Bolton* and the absolute prohibition
present in *Planned Parenthood of Central Missouri v.*

Danforth, and, on the other, the assertedly lesser inhibition imposed by the Connecticut scheme.

. . . . We have repeatedly found that infringements of fundamental rights are not limited to outright denials of those rights. First Amendment decisions have consistently held in a wide variety of contexts that the compelling-state-interest test is applicable not only to outright denials but also to restraints that make exercise of those rights more difficult. . . .

Until today, I had not thought the nature of the fundamental right established in *Roe* was open to question, let alone susceptible of the interpretation advanced by the Court. The fact that the Connecticut scheme may not operate as an absolute bar preventing all indigent women from having abortions is not critical. What is critical is that the State has inhibited their fundamental right to make that choice free from state interference.

. . . . Here . . . Connecticut grants and withholds financial benefits in a manner that discourages significantly the exercise of a fundamental constitutional right. . . . [Roe and Poe] are . . . indigents and therefore even more vulnerable to the financial pressures imposed by the Connecticut regulations.

Belotti v. Baird held, and the Court today agrees, that a state requirement is unconstitutional if it "unduly burdens the right to seek an abortion." Connecticut has "unduly" burdened the fundamental right of pregnant women to be free to choose to have an abortion because the State has advanced no compelling state interest to justify its interference in that choice.

. . . . Finally, the reasons that render the Connecticut regulation unconstitutional also render invalid, in my view, the requirement of a prior written certification by the woman's attending physician that the abortion is "medically necessary," and the requirement that the hospital submit a Request for Authorization of Professional Services including a "statement indicating the medical need for the abortion." For the same reasons, I would also strike down the requirement for prior authorization of payment by the Connecticut Department of Social Services.

JUSTICE MARSHALL dissented. [See the opinion in *Beal v. Doe,* p. 114.]

JUSTICE BLACKMUN (joined by Justices Brennan and Marshall) dissented. [See the opinion in *Beal v. Doe,* p. 117.]

POELKER v. DOE

EXCERPTS

"[W]e find no constitutional violation by the city of St. Louis in electing, as a policy choice, to provide publicly financed hospital services for childbirth without providing corresponding services for nontherapeutic abortions."

Per Curiam [by the Court]

"'Stripped of all rhetoric, the city here, through its policy and staffing procedure, is simply telling indigent women, like Doe, that if they choose to carry their pregnancies to term, the city will provide physicians and medical facilities for full maternity care; but if they choose to exercise their constitutionally protected right to determine that they wish to terminate the pregnancy, the city will not provide physicians and facilities for the abortion procedure, even though it is probably safer than going through a full pregnancy and childbirth.'"

Justice William Brennan

In Brief

Question: May a public hospital refuse to provide elective abortions?

Lower Court: U.S. District Court, Eastern Missouri
U.S. Court of Appeals, Eighth Circuit

Law: Official policy of the Mayor of St. Louis prohibiting abortions in city hospitals

Parties: John Poelker, Mayor, St. Louis, Missouri
Jane Doe, pseudonym of an indigent woman

Counsel: For Poelker: Eugene Freeman
For Doe: Frank Sussman

Arguments: January 11, 1977

Decision: June 20, 1977

Majority: Chief Justice Burger, Justices Stewart, White, Powell, Rehnquist, Stevens

Minority: Justices Brennan, Marshall, Blackmun

Decision by: Per Curiam [by the Court] (p. 139)

Dissents: Justice Brennan (p. 141)
Justice Marshall (see *Beal*, p. 114)
Justice Blackmun (see *Beal*, p. 117)

Offical Text: U.S. Reports, Vol. 432, p. 519
Lower Court: Federal Reporter, Vol. 515, p. 541

THE POELKER COURT

Chief Justice Warren Burger
Appointed 1969 by Richard M. Nixon

Associate Justice William Brennan
Appointed 1956 by Dwight D. Eisenhower

Associate Justice Potter Stewart
Appointed 1958 by Dwight D. Eisenhower

Associate Justice Byron White
Appointed 1962 by John F. Kennedy

Associate Justice Thurgood Marshall
Appointed 1967 by Lyndon B. Johnson

Associate Justice Harry Blackmun
Appointed 1970 by Richard M. Nixon

Associate Justice Lewis Powell
Appointed 1972 by Richard M. Nixon

Associate Justice William Rehnquist
Appointed 1971 by Richard M. Nixon

Associate Justice John Paul Stevens
Appointed 1975 by Gerald R. Ford

POELKER v. DOE

June 20, 1977

PER CURIAM [by the Court]: Respondent Jane Doe, an indigent, sought unsuccessfully to obtain a nontherapeutic abortion at Starkloff Hospital, one of two city-owned public hospitals in St. Louis, Missouri. She subsequently brought this class action [an act on behalf of a group with similar characteristics] . . . against the Mayor of St. Louis and the Director of Health and Hospitals, alleging that the refusal by Starkloff Hospital to provide the desired abortion violated her constitutional rights. . . . [T]he District Court ruled against Doe following a trial[. T]he Court of Appeals for the Eighth Circuit reversed [this decision and] concluded that Doe's inability to obtain an abortion resulted from a combination of a policy directive by the Mayor and a longstanding staffing practice at Starkloff Hospital. The directive, communicated to the Director of Health and Hospitals by the Mayor, prohibited the performance of abortions in the city hospitals except when there was a threat of grave physiological injury or death to the mother. Under the staffing practice, the doctors and medical students at the obstetrics-gynecology clinic at the hospital are drawn from the faculty and students at the St. Louis University School of Medicine, a Jesuit-operated institution opposed to abortion. Relying on our decisions in *Roe v. Wade* and *Doe v. Bolton*, the Court of Appeals held that the city's policy and the hospital's staffing practice denied the "constitutional rights of indigent pregnant women . . . . long after those rights had been clearly enunciated" in *Roe* and *Doe*. The court cast the issue in an equal protection mold, finding that the provision of publicly financed hospital services for childbirth but not for elective abortions constituted invidious discrimination. In support of its equal protection analysis, the court also emphasized the contrast between nonindigent women who can afford to obtain abortions in private hospitals and indigent women who cannot. . . .

[T]he constitutional question presented here is identical in principle with that presented by a State's refusal to provide Medicaid benefits for abortions while providing them for childbirth. This was the issue before us in *Maher v. Roe*. For the reasons set forth in our opinion in that case, we find no constitutional violation by the city of St. Louis in electing, as a policy choice, to provide publicly financed hospital services for childbirth without providing corresponding services for nontherapeutic abortions.

. . . . Although the Mayor's personal [opposing] position on abortion is irrelevant to our decision, we note that he is an elected official responsible to the people of St. Louis. His policy of denying city funds for abortions such as that desired by Doe is subject to public debate and approval or disapproval at the polls. We merely hold, for the reasons stated in *Maher*, that the Constitution does not forbid a State or city, pursuant to democratic processes, from expressing a preference for normal childbirth as St. Louis has done.

The judgment of the Court of Appeals for the Eighth Circuit is reversed, and the case is remanded [returned to the lower court] for further proceedings consistent with this opinion.

It is so ordered.

JUSTICE BRENNAN (joined by Justices Marshall and Blackmun), dissenting: The Court holds that St. Louis may constitutionally refuse to permit the performance of elective abortions in its city-owned hospitals while providing hospital services to women who carry their pregnancies to term. As stated by the Court of Appeals:

> "Stripped of all rhetoric, the city here, through its policy and staffing procedure, is simply telling indigent women, like Doe, that if they choose to carry their pregnancies to term, the city will provide physicians and medical facilities for full maternity care; but if they choose to exercise their constitutionally protected right to determine that they wish to terminate the pregnancy, the city will not provide physicians and facilities for the abortion procedure, even though it is probably safer than going through a full pregnancy and childbirth."

The Court of Appeals held that St. Louis could not in this way "interfer[e] in her decision of whether to bear a child or have an abortion simply because she is indigent and unable to afford private treatment," because it was constitutionally impermissible that indigent women be "'subjected to State coercion to bear children which they do not wish to bear [while] no other women similarly situated are so coerced.'"

For the reasons set forth in my dissent in *Maher v. Roe*, I would affirm the Court of Appeals. Here the fundamental right of a woman freely to choose to terminate her pregnancy has been infringed by the city of St. Louis through a deliberate policy based on opposition to elective abortions on moral grounds by city officials. While it may still be possible for some indigent women to obtain

abortions in clinics or private hospitals, it is clear that the
city policy is a significant, and in some cases insurmount-
able, obstacle to indigent pregnant women who cannot pay
for abortions in those private facilities. Nor is the closing
of St. Louis' public hospitals an isolated instance with little practical significance. The importance of today's decision is greatly magnified by the fact that during 1975 and
the first quarter of 1976 only about 18% of all public
hospitals in the country provided abortion services, and in
10 States there were no public hospitals providing such
services.

A number of difficulties lie beneath the surface of the
Court's holding. Public hospitals that do not permit the
performance of elective abortions will frequently have
physicians on their staffs who would willingly perform
them. This may operate in some communities significantly to reduce the number of physicians who are both willing and able to perform abortions in a hospital setting. It
is not a complete answer that many abortions may safely
be performed in clinics, for some physicians will not be
affiliated with those clinics, and some abortions may pose
unacceptable risks if performed outside a hospital. Indeed, such an answer would be ironic, for if the result is
to force some abortions to be performed in a clinic that
properly should be performed in a hospital, the city policy
will have operated to increase rather than reduce health
risks associated with abortions; and in *Roe v. Wade*, the
Court permitted regulation by the State solely to *protect*
maternal health.

The Court's holding will also pose difficulties in small
communities where the public hospital is the only nearby
health care facility. If such a public hospital is closed to
abortions, any woman - rich or poor - will be seriously in-

convenienced; and for some women - particularly poor women - the unavailability of abortions in the public hospital will be an insuperable obstacle. Indeed, a recent survey suggests that the decision in this case will be felt most strongly in rural areas, where the public hospital will in all likelihood be closed to elective abortions, and where there will not be sufficient demand to support a separate abortion clinic.

Because the city policy constitutes "coercion [of women] to bear children which they do not wish to bear," *Roe v. Wade* and the cases following it require that the city show a compelling state interest that justifies this infringement upon the fundamental right to choose to have an abortion. "[E]xpressing a preference for normal childbirth," does not satisfy that standard. *Roe* explicitly held that during the first trimester no state interest in regulating abortions was compelling, and that during the second trimester the State's interest was compelling only insofar as it protected maternal health. Under *Roe*, the State's "important and legitimate interest in potential life," which I take to be another way of referring to a State's "preference for normal childbirth" - becomes compelling only at the end of the second trimester. Thus it is clear that St. Louis' policy preference is insufficient to justify its infringement on the right of women to choose to have abortions during the first two trimesters of pregnancy without interference by the State on the ground of moral opposition to abortions. St. Louis' policy therefore "unduly burdens the right to seek an abortion."

I would affirm the Court of Appeals.

JUSTICE MARSHALL dissented. [See the opinion in *Beal v. Doe*, p. 114.]

JUSTICE BLACKMUN (joined by Justices Brennan and Marshall) dissented. [See the opinion in *Beal v. Doe*, p. 117.]

COLAUTTI v. FRANKLIN

EXCERPTS

"[A]fter viability, the State, if it chooses, may regulate or even prohibit abortion except where necessary, in appropriate medical judgment, to preserve the life or health of the pregnant woman."

"We hold only that where conflicting duties of this magnitude are involved, the State, at the least, must proceed with greater precision before it may subject a physician to possible criminal sanctions."

Justice Harry Blackmun

"I do not see how it can be seriously argued that a doctor who makes a good-faith mistake about whether a fetus is or is not viable could be successfully prosecuted for criminal homicide."

Justice Byron White

In Brief

Question: Is the Pennsylvania abortion law constitutional?

Lower Court: U.S. District Court, Eastern Pennsylvania

Law: Pennsylvania Abortion Control Act of 1974

Parties: Aldo Colautti, Pennsylvania Secretary of Welfare
                John Franklin, M.D., Director, Planned
                   Parenthood, Southeastern Pennsylvania

Counsel: For Colautti: Carol Los Mansmann
                For Franklin: Roland Morris

Arguments: October 3, 1978

Decision: January 9, 1979

Majority: Justices Brennan, Stewart, Marshall, Blackmun,
                Powell, Stevens

Minority: Chief Justice Burger, Justices White, Rehnquist

Decision by: Justice Blackmun (p. 149)

Dissent: Justice White (p. 161)

Offical Text: U.S. Reports, Vol. 439, p. 379
Lower Court: Federal Supplement, Vol. 401, p. 554

THE COLAUTTI COURT

Chief Justice Warren Burger
Appointed 1969 by Richard M. Nixon

Associate Justice William Brennan
Appointed 1956 by Dwight D. Eisenhower

Associate Justice Potter Stewart
Appointed 1958 by Dwight D. Eisenhower

Associate Justice Byron White
Appointed 1962 by John F. Kennedy

Associate Justice Thurgood Marshall
Appointed 1967 by Lyndon B. Johnson

Associate Justice Harry Blackmun
Appointed 1970 by Richard M. Nixon

Associate Justice Lewis Powell
Appointed 1972 by Richard M. Nixon

Associate Justice William Rehnquist
Appointed 1971 by Richard M. Nixon

Associate Justice John Paul Stevens
Appointed 1975 by Gerald R. Ford

COLAUTTI v. FRANKLIN

January 9, 1979

JUSTICE BLACKMUN: At issue here is the constitutionality of subsection (a) of Section 5 of the Pennsylvania Abortion Control Act. . . .

The Abortion Control Act was passed by the Pennsylvania Legislature, over the Governor's veto, in the year following this Court's decisions in *Roe v. Wade* and *Doe v. Bolton*. It was a comprehensive statute.

Section 1 gave the Act its title. Section 2 defined, among other terms, "informed consent" and "viable." The latter was specified to mean "the capability of a fetus to live outside the mother's womb albeit with artificial aid."

Section 3(a) proscribed the performance of an abortion "upon any person in the absence of informed consent thereto by such person." Section 3(b)(i) prohibited the performance of an abortion in the absence of the written consent of the woman's spouse, provided that the spouse could be located and notified, and the abortion was not certified by a licensed physician "to be necessary in order to preserve the life or health of the mother." Section 3(b)(ii), applicable if the woman was unmarried and under the age of 18, forbade the performance of an abortion in the absence of the written consent of "one parent or person in loco parentis [in place of the parent]" of the woman, unless the abortion was certified by a licensed physician "as necessary in order to preserve the life of the mother." Section 3(e) provided that whoever performed an abortion without such consent was guilty of a misdemeanor of the first degree.

Section 4 provided that whoever, intentionally and willfully, took the life of a premature infant aborted alive, was guilty of murder of the second degree. Section 5(a) . . . provided that if the fetus was determined to be viable, or if there was sufficient reason to believe that the fetus might be viable, the person performing the abortion was required to exercise the same care to preserve the life and health of the fetus as would be required in the case of a fetus intended to be born alive, and was required to adopt the abortion technique providing the best opportunity for the fetus to be aborted alive, so long as a different technique was not necessary in order to preserve the life or health of the mother. Section 5(d) . . . imposed a penal sanction for a violation of Section 5(a).

Section 6 specified abortion controls. It prohibited abortion during the stage of pregnancy subsequent to viability, except where necessary, in the judgment of a licensed physician, to preserve the life or health of the mother. No abortion was to be performed except by a licensed physician and in an approved facility. It required that appropriate records be kept, and that quarterly reports be filed with the Commonwealth's Department of Health. And it prohibited solicitation or advertising with respect to abortions. A violation of Section 6 was a misdemeanor of the first or third degrees, as specified.

Section 7 prohibited the use of public funds for an abortion in the absence of a certificate of a physician stating that the abortion was necessary in order to preserve the life or health of the mother. Finally, Section 8 authorized the Department of Health to make rules and regulations with respect to performance of abortions and the facilities in which abortions were performed.

Prior to the Act's effective date, October 10, 1974, the present suit was filed in the United States District Court for the Eastern District of Pennsylvania challenging, on federal constitutional grounds, nearly all of the Act's provisions. The three-judge court on October 10 issued a preliminary injunction restraining [court order stopping] the enforcement of a number of those provisions. . . .

The case went to trial in January 1975. The court received extensive testimony from expert witnesses on all aspects of abortion procedures. . . . The court sustained the definition of "informed consent" in Section 2; the facility-approval requirement and certain of the reporting requirements of Section 6; Section 8's authorization of rules and regulations; and, by a divided vote, the informed consent requirement of Section 3(a). It overturned Section 3(b)(i)'s spousal-consent requirement and, again by a divided vote, Section 3(b)(ii)'s parental-consent requirement; Section 6's reporting requirements relating to spousal and parental consent; Section 6's prohibition of advertising; and Section 7's restriction on abortion funding. The definition of "viable" in Section 2 was declared void for vagueness and, because of the incorporation of this definition, Section 6's proscription of abortions after viability, except to preserve the life or health of the woman, was struck down. Finally, in part because of the incorporation of the definition of "viable," and in part because of the perceived overbreadth of the phrase "may be viable," the court invalidated the viability-determination and standard-of-care provisions of Section 5(a).

Both sides appealed to this Court. . . .

On remand [return to the lower court], . . . [r]elying on
this Court's supervening decisions in *Beal v. Doe* and
Maher v. Roe, the District Court found, contrary to its
original view, that Section 7 did not violate either Tit[le]
XIX of the Social Security Act . . . or the Equal Protection Clause of the Fourteenth Amendment. The court,
however, declared: "After reconsideration of Section 5(a)
in light of the most recent Supreme Court decisions, we
adhere to our original view and decision that section 5(a)
is unconstitutional." . . . [T]he only issue remaining in this
protracted litigation is the validity of Section 5(a).

Three cases in the sensitive and earnestly contested abortion area provide essential background for the present
controversy.

In *Roe v. Wade*, this Court concluded that there is a right
of privacy, implicit in the liberty secured by the Fourteenth Amendment, that "is broad enough to encompass a
woman's decision whether or not to terminate her pregnancy." This right, we said, although fundamental, is not
absolute or unqualified, and must be considered against
important state interests in the health of the pregnant
woman and in the potential life of the fetus. "These interests are separate and distinct. Each grows in substantiality as the woman approaches term and, at a point during
pregnancy, each becomes 'compelling.'" For both logical
and biological reasons, we indicated that the State's interest in the potential life of the fetus reaches the compelling point at the stage of viability. Hence, prior to viability, the State may not seek to further this interest by directly restricting a woman's decision whether or not to
terminate her pregnancy. But after viability, the State, if
it chooses, may regulate or even prohibit abortion except

where necessary, in appropriate medical judgment, to preserve the life or health of the pregnant woman.

.... We ... left the point [of viability] flexible for anticipated advancements in medical skill.

Roe stressed repeatedly the central role of the physician, both in consulting with the woman about whether or not to have an abortion, and in determining how any abortion was to be carried out. We indicated that up to the points where important state interests provide compelling justifications for intervention, "the abortion decision in all its aspects is inherently, and primarily, a medical decision," and we added that if this privilege were abused, "the usual remedies, judicial and intra-professional, are available."

Roe's companion case, *Doe v. Bolton*, underscored the importance of affording the physician adequate discretion in the exercise of his medical judgment. After the Court there reiterated that "a pregnant woman does not have an absolute constitutional right to an abortion on her demand," the Court discussed . . . the Georgia's statute's requirement that a physician's decision to perform an abortion must rest upon "his best clinical judgment." The Court found it critical that that judgment "may be exercised in the light of all factors - physical, emotional, psychological, familial, and the woman's age - relevant to the well-being of the patient."

The third case, *Planned Parenthood of Central Missouri v. Danforth*, stressed similar themes. There a Missouri statute that defined viability was challenged on the ground that it conflicted with the discussion of viability in *Roe* and that it was, in reality, an attempt to advance the point of viability to an earlier stage in gestation. The Court rejected that argument, repeated the *Roe* definition of viability, and observed again that viability is "a matter of medical judgment, skill, and technical ability, and we preserved [in *Roe*] the flexibility of the term." The Court also rejected a contention that "a specified number of weeks in pregnancy must be fixed by statute as the point of viability." ...

In [*Roe, Doe,* and *Danforth*], then, this Court has stressed viability, has declared its determination to be a matter for medical judgment, and has recognized that differing legal consequences ensue upon the near and far sides of that point in the human gestation period. We reaffirm these principles. Viability is reached when, in the judgment of the attending physician on the particular facts of the case before him, there is a reasonable likelihood of the fetus' sustained survival outside the womb, with or without artificial support. Because this point may differ with each pregnancy, neither the legislature nor the courts may proclaim one of the elements entering into the ascertainment of viability - be it weeks of gestation or fetal wieght or any other single factor - as the determinant of when the State has a compelling interest in the life or health of the fetus. Viability is the critical point. And we have recognized no attempt to stretch the point of viability one way or the other.

With these principles in mind, we turn to the issues presented by the [present] controversy.

.... It is settled that, as a matter of due process, a criminal statute that "fails to give a person of ordinary intelligence fair notice that his contemplated conduct is forbidden by the statute," or is so indefinite that "it encourages arbitrary and erratic arrests and convictions," is void for vagueness. This appears to be especially true where the uncertainty induced by the statute threatens to inhibit the exercise of constitutionally protected rights.

Section 5(a) requires every person who performs or induces an abortion to make a determination, "based on his experience, judgment or professional competence," that the fetus is not viable. If such person determines that the fetus is viable, or if "there is sufficient reason to believe that the fetus may be viable," then he must adhere to the prescribed standard of care. This requirement contains a double ambiguity. First, it is unclear whether the statute imports a purely subjective standard, or whether it imposes a mixed subjective and objective standard. Second, it is uncertain whether the phrase "may be viable" simply refers to viability, as that term has been defined in *Roe* and in *Planned Parenthood,* or whether it refers to an undefined penumbral or "gray" area prior to the stage of viability.

The statute requires the physician to conform to the prescribed standard of care if one of two conditions is satisfied: if he determines that the fetus "is viable," or "if there is sufficient reason to believe that the fetus may be viable." Apparently, the determination of whether the fetus "is viable" is to be based on the attending physician's "experience, judgment or professional competence," a subjective point of reference. But it is unclear whether the same phrase applies to the second triggering condition, that is, to "sufficient reason to believe that the fetus may be viable." In other words, it is ambiguous whether there must be "sufficient reason" from the perspective of the judgment, skill, and training of the attending physician, or "sufficient reason" from the perspective of a cross section of the medical community or a panel of experts. The latter, obviously, portends not an inconsequential hazard for the typical private practitioner who may not have the skills and technology that are readily available at a teaching hospital or large medical center.

The intended distinction between the phrases "is viable" and "may be viable" is even more elusive. . . . The statute . . . does not support the contention that "may be viable" is synonymous with, or merely intended to explicate the meaning of, "viable."

Section 5(a) requires the physician to observe the prescribed standard of care if he determines "that the fetus is viable *or* if there is sufficient reason to believe that the fetus may be viable." The syntax clearly implies that there are two distinct conditions under which the physician must conform to the standard of care. . . .

Furthermore, the suggestion that "may be viable" is an explication of the meaning of "viable" flies in the face of the fact that the statute, in Section 2, already defines "viable." This, presumably, was intended to be the exclusive definition of "viable" throughout the Act. In this respect, it is significant that Section 6(b) of the Act speaks only of the limited availability of abortion during the stage of pregnancy "subsequent to viability." The concept of viability is just as important in Section 6(b) as it is in Section 5(a). Yet in Section 6(b) the legislature found it unnecessary to explain that a "viable" fetus includes one that "may be viable."

Since we must reject [the] theory that "may be viable" means "viable," a second serious ambiguity appears in the statute. On the one hand, . . . as the District Court found, it may be that "may be viable" carves out a new time period during pregnancy when there is a remote possibility of fetal survival outside the womb, but the fetus has not yet attained the reasonable likelihood of survival that physicians associate with viability. On the other hand, . . . it may be that "may be viable" refers to viability as physicians understand it, and "viable" refers to some undetermined stage later in pregnancy. We need not resolve this question. The crucial point is that "viable" and "may be viable" apparently refer to distinct conditions, and that one of these conditions differs in some indeterminate way from the definition of viability as set forth in *Roe* and in *Planned Parenthood.*

Because of the double ambiguity in the viability-determination requirement, this portion of the Pennsylvania statute is readily distinguisable from the requirement that an abortion must be "necessary for the preservation of the mother's life or health," . . . and the requirement that a physician determine, on the basis of his "best clinical judgment," that an abortion is "necessary." . . . The present statute does not afford broad discretion to the physician. Instead, it conditions potential criminal liability on confusing and ambiguous criteria. It therefore presents serious problems of notice, discriminatory application, and chilling effect on the exercise of constitutional rights.

The vagueness of the viability-determination requirement of Section 5(a) is compounded by the fact that the Act subjects the physician to potential criminal liability without regard to fault. Under Section 5(d) . . . a physician who fails to abide by the standard of care when there is sufficient reason to believe that the fetus "may be viable" is subject "to such civil or criminal liability as would pertain to him had the fetus been a child who was intended to be born and not aborted." . . . But neither the Pennsylvania law of criminal homicide, nor the Abortion Control Act, requires that the physician be culpable in failing to find sufficient reason to believe that the fetus may be viable.

. . . . The perils of strict criminal liability are particularly acute here because of the uncertainty of the viability determination itself. As the record in this case indicates, a physician determines whether or not a fetus is viable after considering a number of variables: the gestational age of the fetus, derived from the reported menstrual history of the woman; fetal weight, based on an inexact estimate of the size and condition of the uterus; the woman's general health and nutrition; the quality of the available medical facilities; and other factors. Because of the number and the imprecision of these variables, the probability of any particular fetus' obtaining meaningful life outside the womb can be determined only with difficulty. Moreover, the record indicates that even if agreement may be reached on the probability of survival, different physicians equate viability with different probabilities of survival, and some physicians refuse to equate viability with any numerical probability at all. In the face of these uncertainties, it is not unlikely that experts will disagree over whether a particular fetus in the second trimester has advanced to the stage of viability. The prospect of such disagreement, in conjunction with a statute imposing strict civil and criminal liability for an erroneous determination of viability, could have a profound chilling effect on the willingness of physicians to perform abortions near the point of viability in the manner indicated by their best medical judgment.

Because we hold that the viability-determination provision of Section 5(a) is void . . . , we need not now decide whether, under a properly drafated statute, a finding of bad faith . . . would be required before a physician could be held criminally responsible for an erroneous determination of viability. We reaffirm, however, that "the determination of whether a particular fetus is viable is, and must be, a matter for the judgment of the responsible attending physician." State regulation that impinges upon this determination, if it is to be constitutional, must allow the attending physician "the room he needs to make his best medical judgment."

We also conclude that the standard-of-care provision of Section 5(a) is impermissibly vague. The standard-of-care provision, when it applies, requires the physician to

> "exercise that degree of professional skill, care and diligence to preserve the life and health of the fetus which such person would be required to exercise in order to preserve the life and health of any fetus intended to be born and not aborted and the abortion technique employed shall be that which would provide the best opportunity for the fetus to be aborted alive so long as a different technique would not be necessary in order to preserve the life or health of the mother."

. . . . The District Court took extensive testimony from various physicians about their understanding of this requirement. That testimony is illuminating. When asked what method of abortion they would prefer to use in the second trimester in the absence of Section 5(a), [Colautti's] experts said that they thought saline amnio-infusion was the method of choice. This was described as a method involving removal of amniotic fluid and injec-

tion of a saline or other solution into the amniotic sac.
All physicians agreed, however, that saline amnio-fusion
nearly always is fatal to the fetus, and it was commonly
assumed that this method would be prohibited by the statute.

. . . . Few of the testifying physicians had had any direct
experience with prostaglandins, described as drugs that
stimulate uterine contractibility, inducing premature ex-
pulsion of the fetus. It was generally agreed that the inci-
dence of fetal survival with prostaglandins would be significantly greater than with saline amnio-infusion. Several physicians testified, however, that prostaglandins have
undesirable side effects, such as nausea, vomiting, head-
ache, and diarrhea, and indicated that they are unsafe with
patients having a history of asthma, glaucoma, hyperten-
sion, cardiovascular disease, or epilepsy. . . .

The woman's life and health are not mentioned in the
first part of the stated standard of care, which sets forth
the general duty to the viable fetus; they are mentioned
only in the second part which deals with the choice of
abortion procedures. Moreover, the second part of the
standard directs the physician to employ the abortion
technique best suited to fetal survival "so long as a different technique would not be *necessary* in order to preserve
the life or health of the mother." In this context, the
word "necessary" suggests that a particular technique must
be indispensable to the woman's life or health - not merely desirable - before it may be adopted. And "the life or
health of the mother," as used in Section 5(a), has not
been construed by the courts of the Commonwealth, nor
does it necessarily imply, that all factors relevant to the
welfare of the woman may be taken into account by the
physician in making his decision.

Consequently, it is uncertain whether the statute permits the physician to consider his duty to the patient to be paramount to his duty to the fetus, or whether it requires the physician to make a "trade-off" between the woman's health and additional percentage points of fetal survival. Serious ethical and constitutional difficulties, that we do not address, lurk behind this ambiguity. We hold only that where conflicting duties of this magnitude are involved, the State, at the least, must proceed with greater precision before it may subject a physician to possible criminal sanctions.

. . . . The choice of an appropriate abortion technique, as the record in this case so amply demonstrates, is a complex medical judgment about which experts can - and do - disagree. . . . We conclude that the standard-of-care provision, like the viability-determination requirement, is void for vagueness.

The judgment of the District Court is affirmed [confirmed].

It is so ordered.

JUSTICE WHITE (joined by Chief Justice Burger and Justice Rehnquist), dissenting: . . . . In *Roe v. Wade*, the Court defined the term "viability" to signify the stage at which a fetus is "potentially able to live outside the mother's womb, albeit with artificial aid." This is the point at which the State's interest in protecting fetal life becomes sufficiently strong to permit it to "go so far as to proscribe abortion during that period, except when it is necessary to preserve the life or health of the mother."

The Court obviously crafted its definition of viability
with some care, and it chose to define that term not as
that stage of development at which the fetus actually *is*
able or actually *has* the ability to survive outside the
mother's womb, with or without artificial aid, but as that
point at which the fetus is *potentially* able to survive. In
the ordinary usage of these words, being *able* and being
potentially able do not mean the same thing. Potential
ability is not actual ability. It is [according to *Webster's
Dictionary*] ability "[e]xisting in possibility, not in actuali-
ty." The Court's definition of viability in *Roe v. Wade*
reaches an earlier point in the development of the fetus
than that stage at which a doctor could say with assurance
that the fetus *would* survive outside the womb.

It was against this background that the Pennsylvania statute at issue here was adopted and the District Court's
judgment was entered. Insofar as *Roe v. Wade* was concerned, Pennsylvania could have defined viability in the
language of that case - "potentially able to live outside the
mother's womb" - and could have forbidden all abortions
after this stage of any pregnancy. The Pennsylvania Act,
however, did not go so far. It forbade entirely only those
abortions where the fetus had attained viability as defined
in Section 2 of the Act, that is, where the fetus had "the
capability . . . to live outside the mother's womb albeit
with artificial aid." But the State, understanding that it
also had the power under *Roe v. Wade* to regulate where
the fetus was only "potentially able" to exist outside the
womb, also sought to regulate, but not forbid, abortions
where there was sufficient reason to believe that the fetus
"may be viable"; this language was reasonably believed by
the State to be equivalent to what the Court meant in
1973 by the term "potentially able to live outside the
mother's womb." Under Section 5(a), abortionists must

not only determine whether the fetus is viable but also whether there is sufficient reason to believe that the fetus may be viable. If either condition exists, the method of abortion is regulated and a standard of care imposed. Under Section 5(d), breach of these regulations exposes the abortionist to the civil and criminal penalties that would be applicable if a live birth rather than an abortion had been intended.

. . . . [In *Danforth*], the Court plainly reaffirmed what it had held in *Roe v. Wade*: viability refers not only to that stage of development when the fetus actually has the capability of existing outside the womb but also to that stage when the fetus *may have* the ability to do so. The Court also reaffirmed that at any time after viability, as so understood, the State has the power to prohibit abortions except when necessary to preserve the life or health of the mother.

. . . . In affirming the District Court, the Court does not in so many words agree with the District Court but argues that it is too difficult to know whether the Pennsylvania Act simply intended, as the State urges, to go no further than *Roe* permitted in protecting a fetus that is potentially able to survive or whether it intended to carve out a protected period prior to viability as defined in *Roe*. The District Court, although otherwise seriously in error, had no such trouble with the Act. It understood the "may be viable" provision as an attempt to protect a period of potential life, precisely the kind of interest that *Roe* protected but which the District Court erroneously thought the State was not entitled to protect. *Danforth*, as I have said, reaffirmed *Roe* in this respect. Only those with unalterable determination to invalidate the Pennsylvania Act can draw any measurable difference insofar as vagueness is

concerned between "viability" defined as the ability to
survive and "viability" defined as that stage at which the
fetus may have the ability to survive. It seems to me that,
in affirming, the Court is tacitly disowning the "may be"
standard of the Missouri law as well as the "potential ability" component of viability as that concept was described
in *Roe*. This is a further constitutionally unwarranted intrusion upon the police powers of the States.

. . . . I do not see how it can be seriously argued that a
doctor who makes a good-faith mistake about whether a
fetus is or is not viable could be successfully prosecuted
for criminal homicide. . . . [A]t the very least this is
something the Court should not decide without hearing
from the Pennsylvania courts.

. . . . In any event, I cannot join the Court in its determined attack on the Pennsylvania statute. . . . I agree with
the State that there is not the remotest chance that any
abortionist will be prosecuted on the basis of a good-faith
mistake regarding whether to abort, and if he does, with
respect to which abortion technique is to be used. If there
is substantial doubt about this, the Court should . . . permit the state courts to address the issues in the light of the
Pennsylvania homicide laws with which those courts are
so much more familiar than are we or any other federal
court.

BELLOTTI v. BAIRD

EXCERPTS

"We therefore conclude that if the State decides to require a pregnant minor to obtain one or both parents' consent to an abortion, it also must provide an alternative procedure whereby authorization for the abortion can be obtained."

Justice Lewis Powell

"It is inherent in the right to make the abortion decision that the right may be exercised without public scrutiny and in defiance of the contrary opinion of the sovereign or other third parties."

Justice John Paul Stevens

In Brief

Question: Can Massachusetts require parental consent for a minor's abortion?

Lower Court: U.S. District Court, Massachusetts

Law: Massachusetts General Law, Chapter 112, Section 12S

Parties: Francis Bellotti, Massachusetts Attorney General
William Baird, Director,
  Parents Aid Society

Counsel: For Bellotti: Garrick F. Cole
For Baird: Joseph J. Balliro

Arguments: February 27, 1979

Decision: July 2, 1979

Majority: Chief Justice Burger, Justices Brennan, Stewart, Marshall, Blackmun, Powell, Rehnquist, Stevens

Minority: Justice White

Decision by: Justice Powell (p. 169)

Concurrences: Justice Rehnquist (p. 185)
Justice Stevens (p. 185)

Dissent: Justice White (p. 187)

Offical Text: U.S. Reports, Vol. 443, p. 662
Lower Court: Federal Supplement, Vol. 393, p. 847

THE BELLOTTI COURT

Chief Justice Warren Burger
Appointed 1969 by Richard M. Nixon

Associate Justice William Brennan
Appointed 1956 by Dwight D. Eisenhower

Associate Justice Potter Stewart
Appointed 1958 by Dwight D. Eisenhower

Associate Justice Byron White
Appointed 1962 by John F. Kennedy

Associate Justice Thurgood Marshall
Appointed 1967 by Lyndon B. Johnson

Associate Justice Harry Blackmun
Appointed 1970 by Richard M. Nixon

Associate Justice Lewis Powell
Appointed 1972 by Richard M. Nixon

Associate Justice William Rehnquist
Appointed 1971 by Richard M. Nixon

Associate Justice John Paul Stevens
Appointed 1975 by Gerald R. Ford

BELLOTTI v. BAIRD

July 2, 1979

JUSTICE POWELL (joined by Chief Justice Burger and Justices Stewart and Rehnquist): [This appeal] present[s] a challenge to the constitutionality of a state statute regulating the access of minors to abortions. [It] require[s] us to continue the inquiry we began in *Planned Parenthood of Central Missouri v. Danforth* and *Bellotti v. Baird.*

On August 2, 1974, the Legislature of the Commonwealth of Massachusetts passed, over the Governor's veto, an Act pertaining to abortions performed within the State. According to its title, the statute was intended to regulate abortions "within present constitutional limits." Shortly before the Act was to go into effect, [a] class action [an act taken on behalf of a group with similar characteristics] from which these appeals arise was commenced in the District Court to enjoin [stop], as unconstitutional, the provision of [Section 12S] the Act. . . .

Section 12S provides in part:

"If the mother is less than eighteen years of age and has not married, the consent of both the mother and her parents [to an abortion to be performed on the mother] is required. If one or both of the mother's parents refuse such consent, consent may be obtained by order of a judge of the superior court for good cause shown, after such hearing as he deems necessary. Such a hearing will not require the appointment of a guardian for the mother. If one of the parents has died or has deserted his or her family, consent by the remaining parent is sufficient. If both parents have died or have deserted their family, consent of the mother's guardian or other person having duties similar to a guardian, or any person who had assumed the care and custody of the mother is sufficient. The commissioner of public health shall prescribe a written form for such consent. Such form shall be signed by the proper person or persons and given to the physician performing the abortion who shall maintain it in his permanent files."

Physicians performing abortions in the absence of the consent required by Section 12S are subject to injunctions [court orders to stop an action] and criminal penalties.

A three-judge District Court was convened to hear the case. . . . Plaintiffs in the suit . . . were William Baird; Parents Aid Society, Inc. (Parents Aid), of which Baird is founder and director; Gerald Zupnick, M.D., who regularly performs abortions at the Parents Aid clinic; and an unmarried minor; identified by the pseudonym "Mary Moe," who, at the commencement of the suit, was pregnant, residing at home with her parents, and desirous of obtaining an abortion without informing them.

Mary Moe was permitted to represent the "class of unmarried minors in Massachusetts who have adequate capacity to give a valid and informed consent [to abortion], and who do not wish to involve their parents." . . .

Defendants in the suit . . . were the Attorney General of Massachusetts and the District Attorneys of all counties in the State. Jane Hunerwadel was permitted to intervene as a defendant and representative of the class of Massachusetts parents having unmarried minor daughters who then were, or might become, pregnant. . . .

Following three days of testimony, the District Court issued an opinion invalidating Section 12S. . . .

In its analysis of the relevant constitutional principles the court stated that "there can be no doubt but that a female's constitutional right to an abortion in the first trimester does not depend upon her calendar age." The court found no justification for the parental consent limitation placed on that right by Section 12S, since it concluded that the statute was "cast not in terms of protecting the minor, . . . but in recognizing independent rights of parents." The "independent" parental rights protected by Section 12S, as the court understood them, were wholly distinct from the best interests of the minor.

. . . . We therefore vacated [annulled] the judgment of the District Court, concluding that it should have abstained and certified [sent] to the Supreme Judicial Court of Massachusetts appropriate questions concerning the meaning of Section 12S. . . .

On remand [return to the lower court], the District Court certified nine questions to the Supreme Judicial Court. . . . Among the more important aspects of Section 12S, as authoritatively construed by the Supreme Judicial Court, are the following:

1. In deciding whether to grant consent to their daughter's abortion, parents are required by Section 12S to consider exclusively what will serve her best interests.

2. The provision in Section 12S that judicial consent for an abortion shall be granted, parental objections notwithstanding, "for good cause shown" means that such consent shall be granted if found to be in the minor's best interests. The judge "must disregard all parental objections, and other considerations, which are not based exclusively" on that standard.

3. Even if the judge in a Section 12S proceeding finds "that the minor is capable of making, and has made, an informed and reasonable decision to have an abortion," he is entitled to withhold consent "in circumstances where he determines that the best interests of the minor will not be served by an abortion."

4. As a general rule, a minor who desires an abortion may not obtain judicial consent without first seeking both parents' consent. Exceptions to the rule exist when a parent is not available or when the need for the abortion constitutes "'an emergency requiring immediate action.'" Unless a parent is not available, he must be notified of any judicial proceedings brought under Section 12S.

5. The resolution of Section 12S cases and any appeals that follow can be expected to be prompt. The name of the minor and her parents may be held in confidence. . . .

6. Section 12F which provides, inter alia [among other things], that certain classes of minors may consent to most kinds of medical care without parental approval, does not apply to abortions, except as to minors who are married, widowed, or divorced. Nor does the State's common-law "mature minor rule" create an exception to Section 12S.

Following the judgment of the Supreme Judicial Court,
[Baird] returned to the District Court and obtained a stay
[suspension] of the enforcement of Section 12S until its
constitutionality could be determined. . . . [T]he District
Court again declared Section 12S unconstitutional and en-
joined [stopped] its enforcement.   The court identified
three particular aspects of the statute which, in its view,
rendered it unconstitutional.

First, . . . Section 12S requires parental notice in virtually
every case where the parent is available. The [District]
court believed that the evidence warranted a finding "that
many, perhaps a large majority of 17-year olds are capable of informed consent, as are a not insubstantial number
of 16-year olds, and some even younger." In addition, the
court concluded that it would not be in the best interests
of some "immature" minors - those incapable of giving informed consent - even to inform their parents of their intended abortions. Although the court declined to decide
whether the burden of requiring a minor to take her parents to court was, per se, an impermissible burden on her
right to seek an abortion, it concluded that Massachusetts
could not constitutionally insist that parental permission
be sought or notice given "in those cases where a court, if
given free rein, would find that it was to the minor's best
interests that one or both of her parents not be informed. . . ."

Second, the District Court held that Section 12S was defective in permitting a judge to veto the abortion decision
of a minor found to be capable of giving informed consent. The court reasoned that upon a finding of maturity
and informed consent, the State no longer was entitled to
impose legal restrictions upon this decision. Given such a
finding, the court could see "no reasonable basis" for dis-

tinguishing between a minor and an adult, and it therefore concluded that Section 12S was not only "an undue burden in the due process sense, [but] a discriminatory denial of equal protection [as well]."

Finally, the court decided that Section 12S suffered from what it termed "formal overbreadth" because the statute failed explicitly to inform parents that they must consider only the minor's best interests in deciding whether to grant consent. The court believed that, despite the Supreme Judicial Court's construction of Section 12S, parents naturally would infer from the statute that they were entitled to withhold consent for other, impermissible reasons. This was thought to create a "chilling effect" by enhancing the possibility that parental consent would be denied wrongfully and that the minor would have to proceed in court.

. . . . The District Court . . . adhered to its previous position, declaring Section 12S unconstitutional and permanently [stopping] its enforcement. [Bellotti] sought review in this Court a second time. . . .

A child, merely on account of his minority, is not beyond the protection of the Constitution. As the Court said in [Gault], "whatever may be their precise impact, neither the Fourteenth Amendment nor the Bill of Rights is for adults alone." This observation, of course, is but the beginning of the analysis. The Court long has recognized that the status of minors under the law is unique in many respects. As Justice Frankfurter aptly put it: "Children have a very special place in life which law should reflect. Legal theories and their phrasing in other cases readily lead to fallacious reasoning if uncritically transferred to determination of a State's duty towards children." The unique role in our society of the family, the institution by which "we inculcate and pass down many of our most cherished values, moral and cultural," requires that constitutional principles be applied with sensitivity and flexibility to the special needs of parents and children. We have recognized three reasons justifying the conclusion that the constitutional rights of children cannot be equated with those of adults: the peculiar vulnerability of children; their inability to make critical decisions in an informed, mature manner; and the importance of the parental role in child rearing.

The Court's concern for the vulnerability of children is demonstrated in its decisions dealing with minors' claims to constitutional protection against deprivations of liberty or property interests by the State. With respect to many of these claims, we have concluded that the child's right is virtually coextensive with that of an adult. For example, the Court has held that the Fourteenth Amendment's guarantee against the deprivation of liberty without due process of law is applicable to children in juvenile delinquency proceedings. In particular, minors involved in such proceedings are entitled to adequate notice, the assistance of counsel, and the opportunity to confront their accusers. They can be found guilty only upon proof beyond a reasonable doubt, and they may assert the privilege against compulsory self-incrimination. Similarly, in *Goss v. Lopez*, the Court held that children may not be deprived of certain property interests without due process.

These rulings have not been made on the uncritical assumption that the constitutional rights of children are undistinguishable from those of adults. Indeed, our acceptance of juvenile courts distinct from the adult criminal justice system assumes that juvenile offenders constitu-

tionally may be treated differently from adults. In order
to preserve this separate avenue for dealing with minors,
the Court has said that hearings in juvenile delinquency
cases need not necessarily "'conform with all of the requirements of a criminal trial or even of the usual admin-
istrative hearing.'" Thus, juveniles are not constitutionally entitled to trial by jury in delinquency adjudications.
Viewed together, our cases show that although children
generally are protected by the same constitutional guarantees against governmental deprivations as are adults, the
State is entitled to adjust its legal system to account for
children's vulnerability and their needs for "concern, . . .
sympathy, and . . . paternal attention."

Second, the Court has held that the States validly may limit the freedom of children to choose for themselves in the
making of important, affirmative choices with potentially
serious consequences. These rulings have been grounded
in the recognition that, during the formative years of
childhood and adolescence, minors often lack the experience, perspective, and judgment to recognize and avoid
choices that could be detrimental to them.

Ginsburg v. New York illustrates well the Court's concern
over the inability of children to make mature choices, as
the First Amendment rights involved are clear examples
of constitutionally protected freedoms of choice. At issue
was a criminal conviction for selling sexually oriented
magazines to a minor under the age of 17 in violation of a
New York state law. It was conceded that the conviction
could not have stood under the First Amendment if based
upon a sale of the same material to an adult. Notwithstanding the importance the Court always has attached to
First Amendment rights, it concluded that "even where
there is an invasion of protected freedoms 'the power of

the state to control the conduct of children reaches beyond the scope of its authority over adults. . . .'" The Court was convinced that the New York Legislature rationally could conclude that the sale to children of the magazines in question presented a danger against which they should be guarded. It therefore rejected the argument that the New York Law violated the constitutional rights of minors.

Third, the guiding role of parents in the upbringing of their children justifies limitations on the freedoms of minors. The State commonly protects its youth from adverse governmental action and from their own immaturity by requiring parental consent to or involvement in important decisions by minors. But an additional and more important justification for state deference to parental control over children is that "[t]he child is not the mere creature of the State; those who nurture him and direct his destiny have the right, coupled with the high duty, to recognize and prepare him for additional obligations." "The duty to prepare the child for 'additional obligations' . . . must be read to include the inculcation of moral standards, religious beliefs, and elements of good citizenship." This affirmative process of teaching, guiding, and inspiring by precept and example is essential to the growth of young people into mature, socially responsible citizens.

We have believed in this country that this process, in large part, is beyond the competence of impersonal political institutions. Indeed, affirmative sponsorship of particular ethical, religious, or political beliefs is something we expect the State *not* to attempt in a society constitutionally committed to the ideal of individual liberty and freedom of choice. Thus, "[i]t is cardinal with us that the custody, care and nurture of the child reside first in the parents, whose primary function and freedom include *preparation for obligations the state can neither supply nor hinder."*

. . . . [T]he tradition of parental authority is not inconsistent with our tradition of individual liberty; rather, the former is one of the basic presuppositions of the latter. Legal restrictions on minors, especially those supportive of the parental role, may be important to the child's chances for the full growth and maturity that make eventual participation in a free society meaningful and rewarding. Under the Constitution, the State can "properly conclude that parents and others, teachers for example, who have [the] primary responsibility for children's well-being are entitled to the support of laws designed to aid discharge of that responsibility."

With these principles in mind, we consider the specific constitutional questions presented by these appeals. In Section 12S, Massachusetts has attempted to reconcile the constitutional right of a woman, in consultation with her physician, to choose to terminate her pregnancy as established by *Roe v. Wade* and *Doe v. Bolton*, with the special interest of the State in encouraging an unmarried pregnant minor to seek the advice of her parents in making the important decision whether or not to bear a child. . . . The question before us - in light of what we have said in . . . prior cases - is whether Section 12S, as authoritatively interpreted by the [Massachusetts] Supreme Judicial Court, provides for parental notice and consent in a manner that does not unduly burden the right to seek an abortion.

. . . . As immature minors often lack the ability to make fully informed choices that take account of both immediate and long-range consequences, a State reasonably may determine that parental consultation often is desirable and in the best interest of the minor. It may further determine, as a general proposition, that such consultation is particularly desirable with respect to the abortion decision - one that for some people raises profound moral and religious concerns. . . .

[W]e are concerned here with a constitutional right to seek an abortion. The abortion decision differs in important ways from other decisions that may be made during minority. The need to preserve the constitutional right and the unique nature of the abortion decision, especially when made by a minor, require a State to act with particular sensitivity when it legislates to foster parental involvement in this matter.

The pregnant minor's options are much different from those facing a minor in other situations, such as deciding whether to marry. A minor not permitted to marry before the age of majority is required simply to postpone her decision. She and her intended spouse may preserve the opportunity for later marriage should they continue to desire it. A pregnant adolescent, however, cannot preserve for long the possibility of aborting, which effectively expires in a matter of weeks from the onset of pregnancy.

Moreover, the potentially severe detriment facing a pregnant woman is not mitigated by her minority. Indeed, considering her probable education, employment skills, financial resources, and emotional maturity, unwanted motherhood may be exceptionally burdensome for a minor. In addition, the fact of having a child brings with it adult legal responsibility, for parenthood, like attainment of the age of majority, is one of the traditional criteria for the termination of the legal disabilities of minority. In sum, there are few situations in which denying a minor the right to make an important decision will have consequences so grave and indelible.

Yet, an abortion may not be the best choice for the minor. The circumstances in which this issue arises will vary widely. In a given case, alternatives to abortion, such as marriage to the father of the child, arranging for its adoption, or assuming the responsibilities of motherhood with the assured support of family, may be feasible and relevant to the minor's best interests. Nonetheless, the abortion decision is one that simply cannot be postponed, or it will be made by default with far-reaching consequences.

For these reasons, as we held in *Planned Parenthood of Missouri v. Danforth*, "the State may not impose a blanket provision . . . requiring the consent of a parent or person in loco parentis [in place of the parent] as a condition for abortion of an unmarried minor during the first 12 weeks of her pregnancy." Although . . . such deference to parents may be permissible with respect to other choices facing a minor, the unique nature and consequences of the abortion decision make it inappropriate "to give a third party an absolute, and possibly arbitrary, veto over the decision of the physician and his patient to terminate the patient's pregnancy, regardless of the reason for withholding the consent." We therefore conclude that if the State decides to require a pregnant minor to obtain one or both parents' consent to an abortion, it also must provide an alternative procedure whereby authorization for the abortion can be obtained.

A pregnant minor is entitled in such a proceeding to show either: (1) that she is mature enough and well enough informed to make her abortion decision, in consultation with her physician, independently of her parents' wishes; or (2) that even if she is not able to make this decision independently, the desired abortion would be in her best interests. The proceeding in which this showing is made must assure that a resolution of the issue, and any appeals that may follow, will be completed with anonymity and sufficient expedition to provide an effective opportunity for an abortion to be obtained. In sum, the procedure must ensure that the provision requiring parental consent does not in fact amount to the "absolute, and possibly arbitrary, veto" that was found impermissible in *Danforth*.

It is against these requirements that Section 12S must be tested. . . .

Among the questions [sent] to the Supreme Judicial Court was whether Section 12S permits any minors - mature or immature, to obtain judicial consent to an abortion without any parental consultation whatsoever. The state court answered that, in general, it does not. . . .

We think that . . . Section 12S would impose an undue burden upon the exercise by minors of the right to seek an abortion. As the District Court recognized, "there are parents who would obstruct, and perhaps altogether prevent, the minor's right to go to court." There is no reason to believe that this would be so in the majority of cases where consent is withheld. But many parents hold strong views on the subject of abortion, and young pregnant minors, especially those living at home, are particularly vulnerable to their parents' efforts to obstruct both an abor-

tion and their access to court. It would be unrealistic,
therefore, to assume that the mere existence of a legal
right to seek relief in superior court provides an effective
avenue of relief for some of those who need it the most.

We conclude, therefore, that under state regulation such
as that undertaken by Massachusetts, every minor must
have the opportunity - if she so desires - to go directly to
a court without first consulting or notifying her parents.
If she satisfies the court that she is mature and well
enough informed to make intelligently the abortion decision on her own, the court must authorize her to act without parental consultation or consent. If she fails to satisfy
the court that she is competent to make this decision independently, she must be permitted to show that an abortion
nevertheless would be in her best interests. If the court is
persuaded that it is, the court must authorize the abortion.
If, however, the court is not persuaded by the minor that
she is mature or that the abortion would be in her best interests, it may decline to sanction the operation.

There is, however, an important state interest in encouraging a family rather than a judicial resolution of a minor's
abortion decision. Also, as we have observed above, parents naturally take an interest in the welfare of their children - an interest that is particularly strong where a normal family relationship exists and where the child is living with one or both parents. These factors properly may
be taken into account by a court called upon to determine
whether an abortion in fact is in a minor's best interests.
If, all things considered, the court determines that an
abortion is in the minor's best interests, she is entitled to
court authorization without any parental involvement.
On the other hand, the court may deny the abortion request of an immature minor in the absence of parental

consultation if it concludes that her best interests would be served thereby, or the court may in such a case defer decision until there is parental consultation in which the court may participate. But this is the full extent to which parental involvement may be required. For the reasons stated above, the constitutional right to seek an abortion may not be unduly burdened by state-imposed conditions upon initial access to court.

Section 12S requires that both parents consent to a minor's abortion. . . .

We are not persuaded that, as a general rule, the requirement of obtaining both parents' consent unconstitutionally burdens a minor's right to seek an abortion. The abortion decision has implications far broader than those associated with most other kinds of medical treatment. . . . Consent and involvement by parents in important decisions by minors long have been recognized as protective of their immaturity. In the case of the abortion decision, for reasons we have stated, the focus of the parents' inquiry should be the best interests of their daughter. As every pregnant minor is entitled in the first instance to go directly to the court for a judicial determination without prior parental notice, consultation, or consent, the general rule with respect to parental consent does not unduly burden the constitutional right. Moreover, where the pregnant minor goes to her parents and consent is denied, she still must have recourse to a prompt judicial determination of her maturity or best interests.

Another of the questions [sent] by the District Court to the Supreme Judicial Court was the following: "If the superior court finds that the minor is capable [of making], and has, in fact, made and adhered to, an informed and reasonable decision to have an abortion, may the court refuse its consent based on a finding that a parent's, or its own, contrary decision is a better one?" . . .

The Supreme Judicial Court's statement reflects the general rule that a State may require a minor to wait until the age of majority before being permitted to exercise legal rights independently. But we are concerned here with the exercise of a constitutional right of unique character. . . . [I]f the minor satisfies a court that she has attained sufficient maturity to make a fully informed decision, she then is entitled to make her abortion decision independently. We therefore agree with the District Court that Section 12S cannot constitutionally permit judicial disregard of the abortion decision of a minor who has been determined to be mature and fully competent to assess the implications of the choice she has made.

Although it satisfies constitutional standards in large part, Section 12S falls short of them in two respects: First, it permits judicial authorization for an abortion to be withheld from a minor who is found by the superior court to be mature and fully competent to make this decision independently. Second, it requires parental consultation or notification in every instance, without affording the pregnant minor an opportunity to receive an independent judicial determination that she is mature enough to consent or that an abortion would be in her best interests. Accordingly, we affirm the judgment of the District Court insofar as it invalidates this statute and [stops] its enforcement.

Affirmed.

JUSTICE REHNQUIST, concurring: I join the opinion of Justice Powell and the judgment of the Court. At such time as this Court is willing to reconsider its earlier decision in *Planned Parenthood of Central Missouri v. Danforth*, in which I joined the opinion of Justice White, dissenting in part, I shall be more than willing to participate in that task. But unless and until that time comes, literally thousands of judges cannot be left with nothing more than the guidance offered by a truly fragmented holding of this Court.

JUSTICE STEVENS (joined by Justices Brennan, Marshall, and Blackmun), concurring in the judgment: In *Roe v. Wade*, the Court held that a woman's right to decide whether to terminate a pregnancy is entitled to constitutional protection. In *Planned Parenthood of Central Missouri v. Danforth*, the Court held that a pregnant minor's right to make the abortion decision may not be conditioned on the consent of one parent. I am persuaded that these decisions require affirmance [confirmation] of the District Court's holding that the Massachusetts statute is unconstitutional.

The Massachusetts statute is, on its face, simple and straightforward. It provides that every woman under 18 who has not married must secure the consent of both her parents before receiving an abortion. "If one or both of the mother's parents refuse such consent, consent may be obtained by order of a judge of the superior court for good cause shown."

Whatever confusion or uncertainty might have existed as to how this statute was to operate has been eliminated by the authoritative construction of its provisions by the Massachusetts Supreme Judicial Court. The statute was

construed to require that every minor who wishes an
abortion must first seek the consent of both parents, unless a parent is not available or unless the need for the
abortion constitutes "'an emergency requiring immediate
action.'" ... [N]o minor in Massachusetts, no matter how
mature and capable of informed decisionmaking, may receive an abortion without the consent of either both her
parents or a superior court judge. In every instance, the
minor's decision to secure an abortion is subject to an absolute third-party veto.

In *Planned Parenthood of Central Missouri v. Danforth*,
this Court invalidated statutory provisions requiring the
consent of the husband of a married woman and of one
parent of a pregnant minor to an abortion.... Unlike the
Missouri statute [in *Danforth*], Massachusetts requires the
consent of both of the woman's parents. It does, of
course, provide an alternative in the form of a suit initiated by the woman in superior court. But in that proceeding, the judge is afforded an absolute veto over the
minor's decisions, based on his judgment of her best interests. In Massachusetts, then, as in Missouri, the State has
imposed an "absolute limitation on the minor's right to
obtain an abortion," applicable to every pregnant minor in
the State who has not married.

The provision of an absolute veto to a judge - or, potentially, to an appointed administrator - is to me particularly
troubling. The constitutional right to make the abortion
decision affords protection to both of the privacy interests recognized in this Court's cases: "One is the individual interest in avoiding disclosure of personal matters, and
another is the interest in independence in making certain
kinds of important decisions." It is inherent in the right
to make the abortion decision that the right may be exer-

cised without public scrutiny and in defiance of the contrary opinion of the sovereign or other third parties. In Massachusetts, however, every minor who cannot secure the consent of both her parents - which under *Danforth* cannot be an absolute prerequisite to an abortion - is required to secure the consent of the sovereign. As a practical matter, I would suppose that the need to commence judicial proceedings in order to obtain a legal abortion would impose a burden at least as great as, and probably greater than, that imposed on the minor child by the need to obtain the consent of a parent. Moreover, once this burden is met, the only standard provided for the judge's decision is the best interest of the minor. That standard provides little real guidance to the judge, and his decision must necessarily reflect personal and societal values and mores whose enforcement upon the minor - particularly when contrary to her own informed and reasonable decision - is fundamentally at odds with privacy interests underlying the constitutional protection afforded to her decision.

In short, it seems to me that this case is governed by *Danforth*; to the extent this statute differs from that in *Danforth*, it is potentially even more restrictive of the constitutional right to decide whether or not to terminate a pregnancy. . . .

JUSTICE WHITE, dissenting: I was in dissent in *Planned Parenthood of Central Missouri v. Danforth* on the issue of the validity of requiring the consent of a parent when an unmarried woman under 18 years of age seeks an abortion. I continue to have the views I expressed there. . . . I would not, therefore, strike down this Massachusetts law.

. . . . Until now, I would have thought inconceivable a

holding that the United States Constitution forbids even notice to parents when their minor child who seeks surgery objects to such notice and is able to convince a judge that the parents should be denied participation in the decision.

With all due respect, I dissent.

THE U.S. CONSTITUTION

THE U.S. CONSTITUTION

PREAMBLE

We the people of the United States, in order to form a more perfect union, establish justice, insure domestic tranquility, provide for the common defense, promote the general welfare, and secure the blessings of liberty to ourselves and our posterity, do ordain and establish this Constitution for the United States of America.

ARTICLE I

Section 1. All legislative powers herein granted shall be vested in a Congress of the United States, which shall consist of a Senate and House of Representatives.

Section 2. (1) The House of Representatives shall be composed of members chosen every second year by the people of the several states, and the electors in each state shall have the qualifications requisite for electors of the most numerous branch of the State Legislature.

(2) No person shall be a Representative who shall not have attained to the age of twenty-five years, and been seven years a citizen of the United States, and who shall not, when elected, be an inhabitant of that state in which he shall be chosen.

(3) Representatives and direct taxes shall be apportioned among the several states which may be included within this union, according to their respective numbers, which shall be determined by adding to the whole number of free persons, including those bound to service for a term of years, and excluding Indians not taxed, three-fifths of all other persons. The actual enumeration shall be made

within three years after the first meeting of the Congress of the United States, and within every subsequent term of ten years, in such manner as they shall by law direct. The number of Representatives shall not exceed one for every thirty thousand, but each state shall have at least one Representative; and until such enumeration shall be made, the State of New Hampshire shall be entitled to choose three, Massachusetts eight, Rhode Island and Providence Plantations one, Connecticut five, New York six, New Jersey four, Pennsylvania eight, Delaware one, Maryland six, Virginia ten, North Carolina five, South Carolina five, and Georgia three.

(4) When vacancies happen in the representation from any state, the executive authority thereof shall issue writs of election to fill such vacancies.

(5) The House of Representatives shall choose their Speaker and other Officers; and shall have the sole power of impeachment.

Section 3. (1) The Senate of the United States shall be composed of two Senators from each state, chosen by the legislature thereof, for six years; and each Senator shall have one vote.

(2) Immediately after they shall be assembled in consequence of the first election, they shall be divided as equally as may be into three classes. The seats of the Senators of the first class shall be vacated at the expiration of the second year, of the second class at the expiration of the fourth year, and of the third class at the expiration of the sixth year, so that one-third may be chosen every second year; and if vacancies happen by resignation, or otherwise, during the recess of the legislature of any state, the execu-

tive thereof may make temporary appointments until the next meeting of the legislature, which shall then fill such vacancies.

(3) No person shall be a Senator who shall not have attained to the age of thirty years, and been nine years a citizen of the United States, and who shall not, when elected, be an inhabitant of that state for which he shall be chosen.

(4) The Vice President of the United States shall be President of the Senate, but shall have no vote, unless they be equally divided.

(5) The Senate shall choose their other Officers, and also a President pro tempore, in the absence of the Vice President, or when he shall exercise the Office of President of the United States.

(6) The Senate shall have the sole power to try all impeachments. When sitting for that purpose, they shall be on oath or affirmation. When the President of the United States is tried, the Chief Justice shall preside: and no person shall be convicted without the concurrence of two-thirds of the members present.

(7) Judgment in cases of impeachment shall not extend further than to removal from office, and disqualification to hold and enjoy any office of honor, trust, or profit under the United States: but the party convicted shall nevertheless be liable and subject to indictment, trial, judgment, and punishment, according to law.

Section 4. (1) The times, places and manner of holding elections for Senators and Representatives, shall be prescribed in each state by the legislature thereof; but the Congress may at any time by law make or alter such regulations, except as to the places of choosing Senators.

(2) The Congress shall assemble at least once in every year, and such meeting shall be on the first Monday in December, unless they shall by law appoint a different day.

Section 5. (1) Each House shall be the judge of the elections, returns, and qualifications of its own members, and a majority of each shall constitute a quorum to do business; but a smaller number may adjourn from day to day, and may be authorized to compel the attendance of absent members, in such manner, and under such penalties as each House may provide.

(2) Each House may determine the rules of its proceedings, punish its members for disorderly behavior, and, with the concurrence of two-thirds, expel a member.

(3) Each House shall keep a journal of its proceedings, and from time to time publish the same, excepting such parts as may in their judgment require secrecy; and the yeas and nays of the members of either House on any question shall, at the desire of one-fifth of those present, be entered on the journal.

(4) Neither House, during the Session of Congress, shall, without the consent of the other, adjourn for more than three days, nor to any other place than that in which the two Houses shall be sitting.

Section 6. (1) The Senators and Representatives shall receive a compensation for their services, to be ascertained by law, and paid out of the Treasury of the United States. They shall in all cases, except treason, felony and breach of the peace, be privileged from arrest during their attendance at the session of their respective Houses, and in going to and returning from the same; and for any speech or debate in either House, they shall not be questioned in any other place.

(2) No Senator or Representative shall, during the time for which he was elected, be appointed to any civil office under the authority of the United States, which shall have been created, or the emoluments whereof shall have been increased during such time and no person holding any office under the United States, shall be a member of either House during his continuance in office.

Section 7. (1) All bills for raising revenue shall originate in the House of Representatives; but the Senate may propose or concur with amendments as on other bills.

(2) Every bill which shall have passed the House of Representatives and the Senate, shall, before it become a law, be presented to the President of the United States; if he approve he shall sign it, but if not he shall return it, with his objections to the House in which it shall have originated, who shall enter the objections at large on their journal, and proceed to reconsider it. If after such reconsideration two-thirds of that House shall agree to pass the bill, it shall be sent together with the objections, to the other House, by which it shall likewise be reconsidered, and if approved by two-thirds of that House, it shall become a law. But in all such cases the votes of both Houses shall be determined by yeas and nays, and the names of the per-

sons voting for and against the bill shall be entered on the journal of each House respectively. If any bill shall not be returned by the President within ten days (Sundays excepted) after it shall have been presented to him, the same shall be a law, in like manner as if he had signed it, unless the Congress by their adjournment prevent its return in which case it shall not be a law.

(3) Every order, resolution, or vote, to which the concurrence of the Senate and House of Representatives may be necessary (except on a question of adjournment) shall be presented to the President of the United States; and before the same shall take effect, shall be approved by him, or being disapproved by him, shall be repassed by two-thirds of the Senate and House of Representatives, according to the rules and limitations prescribed in the case of a bill.

Section 8. (1) The Congress shall have the power to lay and collect taxes, duties, imposts and excises, to pay the debts and provide for the common defense and general welfare of the United States; but all duties, imposts and excises shall be uniform throughout the United States;

(2) To borrow money on the credit of the United States;

(3) To regulate commerce with foreign nations, and among the several states, and with the Indian Tribes;

(4) To establish an uniform Rule of Naturalization, and uniform laws on the subject of bankruptcies throughout the United States;

(5) To coin money, regulate the value thereof, and of foreign coin, and fix the standard of weights and measures;

(6) To provide for the punishment of counterfeiting the securities and current coin of the United States;

(7) To establish Post Offices and Post Roads;

(8) To promote the progress of science and useful arts, by securing for limited times to authors and inventors the exclusive right to their respective writings and discoveries;

(9) To constitute tribunals inferior to the Supreme Court;

(10) To define and punish piracies and felonies committed on the high seas, and offenses against the Law of Nations;

(11) To declare war, grant Letters of marque and reprisal, and make rules concerning captures on land and water;

(12) To raise and support armies, but no appropriation of money to that use shall be for a longer term than two years;

(13) To provide and maintain a Navy;

(14) To make rules for the government and regulation of the land and naval forces;

(15) To provide for calling forth the Militia to execute the laws of the Union, suppress insurrections and repel invasions;

(16) To provide for organizing, arming, and disciplining, the Militia, and for governing such part of them as may be employed in the service of the United States, reserving to the states respectively, the appointment of the Officers,

and the authority of training the Militia according to the discipline prescribed by Congress;

(17) To exercise exclusive legislation in all cases whatsoever, over such district (not exceeding ten miles square) as may, by cession of particular states, and the acceptance of Congress, become the Seat of the Government of the United States, and to exercise like authority over all places purchased by the consent of the legislature of the state in which the same shall be, for the erection of forts, magazines, arsenals, dockyards, and other needful buildings; - and

(18) To make all laws which shall be necessary and proper for carrying into execution the foregoing powers, and all other powers vested by this Constitution in the Government of the United States, or in any Department or Officer thereof.

Section 9. (1) The migration or importation of such persons as any of the states now existing shall think proper to admit, shall not be prohibited by the Congress prior to the year one thousand eight hundred and eight, but a tax or duty may be imposed on such importation, not exceeding ten dollars for each person.

(2) The privilege of the writ of habeas corpus shall not be suspended, unless when in cases of rebellion or invasion the public safety may require it.

(3) No bill of attainder or ex post facto law shall be passed.

(4) No capitation, or other direct, tax shall be laid, unless in proportion to the census or enumeration herein before directed to be taken.

(5) No tax or duty shall be laid on articles exported from any state.

(6) No preference shall be given by any regulation of commerce or revenue to the ports of one state over those of another: nor shall vessels bound to, or from, one state be obliged to enter, clear, or pay duties in another.

(7) No money shall be drawn from the Treasury, but in consequence of appropriations made by law; and a regular statement and account of the receipts and expenditures of all public money shall be published from time to time.

(8) No title of nobility shall be granted by the United States: and no person holding any office of profit or trust under them, shall, without the consent of the Congress, accept of any present, emolument, office, or title, of any kind whatever, from any King, Prince, or foreign State.

Section 10. (1) No state shall enter into any treaty, alliance, or confederation; grant letters of marque and reprisal; coin money; emit bills of credit; make any thing but gold and silver coin a tender in payment of debts; pass any bill of attainder, ex post facto law, or law impairing the obligation of contracts, or grant any title of nobility.

(2) No state shall, without the consent of the Congress, lay any imposts or duties on imports or exports, except what may be absolutely necessary for executing its inspection laws: and the net produce of all duties and imposts, laid by any state on imports or exports, shall be for the use of

the Treasury of the United States; and all such laws shall
be subject to the revision and control of the Congress.

(3) No state shall, without the consent of Congress, lay
any duty of tonnage, keep troops, or ships of war in time
of peace, enter into any agreement or compact with another state, or with a foreign power, or engage in war, unless
actually invaded, or in such imminent danger as will not
admit of delay.

ARTICLE II

Section 1. (1) The executive power shall be vested in a
President of the United States of America. He shall hold
his office during the term of four years, and, together
with the Vice President, chosen for the same term, be
elected, as follows:

(2) Each state shall appoint, in such manner as the legislature thereof may direct, a number of electors, equal to the
whole number of Senators and Representatives to which
the state may be entitled in the Congress; but no Senator
or Representative, or person holding an office of trust or
profit under the United States, shall be appointed an Elector.

(3) The electors shall meet in their respective states, and
vote by ballot for two persons, of whom one at least shall
not be an inhabitant of the same state with themselves.
And they shall make a list of all the persons voted for,
and of the number of votes for each; which list they shall
sign and certify, and transmit sealed to the Seat of the
Government of the United States, directed to the President of the Senate. The President of the Senate shall, in
the presence of the Senate and House of Representatives,

open all the certificates, and the votes shall then be counted. The person having the greatest number of votes shall
be the President, if such number be a majority of the
whole number of electors appointed; and if there be more
than one who have such majority, and have an equal number of votes, then the House of Representatives shall immediately choose by ballot one of them for President; and
if no person have a majority, then from the five highest
on the list the said House shall in like manner choose the
President. But in choosing the President, the votes shall
be taken by states the representation from each state having one vote; a quorum for this purpose shall consist of a
member or members from two-thirds of the states, and a
majority of all the states shall be necessary to a choice. In
every case, after the choice of the President, the person
having the greater number of votes of the electors shall
be the Vice President. But if there should remain two or
more who have equal votes, the Senate shall choose from
them by ballot the Vice President.

(4) The Congress may determine the time of choosing the
Electors, and the day on which they shall give their votes;
which day shall be the same throughout the United States.

(5) No person except a natural born citizen, or a citizen of
the United States, at the time of the adoption of this Constitution, shall be eligible to the Office of President; neither shall any person be eligible to that Office who shall
not have attained to the age of thirty-five years, and been
fourteen years a resident within the United States.

(6) In case of the removal of the President from Office,
or of his death, resignation or inability to discharge the
powers and duties of the said Office, the same shall devolve on the Vice President, and the Congress may by law

provide for the case of removal, death, resignation or inability, both of the President and Vice President, declaring
what Officer shall then act as President, and such Officer
shall act accordingly, until the disability be removed, or a
President shall be elected.

(7) The President shall, at stated times, receive for his
services, a compensation, which shall neither be increased
nor diminished during the period for which he shall have
been elected, and he shall not receive within that period
any other emolument from the United States, or any of
them.

(8) Before he enter on the execution of his office, he shall
take the following oath or affirmation: "I do solemnly
swear (or affirm) that I will faithfully execute the Office
of President of the United States, and will to the best of
my ability, preserve, protect and defend the Constitution
of the United States."

Section 2. (1) The President shall be Commander in Chief
of the Army and Navy of the United States, and of the
militia of the several states, when called into the actual
service of the United States; he may require the opinion,
in writing, of the principal Officer in each of the Executive Departments, upon any subject relating to the duties
of their respective Offices, and he shall have power to
grant reprieves and pardons for offenses against the United States, except in cases of impeachment.

(2) He shall have power, by and with the advice and consent of the Senate to make treaties, provided two-thirds of
the Senators present concur; and he shall nominate, and
by and with the advice and consent of the Senate, shall appoint Ambassadors, other public Ministers and Consuls,

Judges of the supreme Court, and all other Officers of the United States, whose appointments are not herein otherwise provided for, and which shall be established by law; but the Congress may by law vest the appointment of such inferior Officers, as they think proper, in the President alone, in the courts of law, or in the heads of departments.

(3) The President shall have power to fill up all vacancies that may happen during the recess of the Senate, by granting commissions which shall expire at the end of their next session.

Section 3. He shall from time to time give to the Congress information of the State of the Union, and recommend to their consideration such measures as he shall judge necessary and expedient; he may, on extraordinary occasions, convene both Houses, or either of them, and in case of disagreement between them, with respect to the time of adjournment, he may adjourn them to such time as he shall think proper; he shall receive Ambassadors and other public Ministers; he shall take care that the laws be faithfully executed, and shall commission all the Officers of the United States.

Section 4. The President, Vice President and all civil Officers of the United States, shall be removed from office on impeachment for, and conviction of, treason, bribery, or other high crimes and misdemeanors.

ARTICLE III

Section 1. The judicial power of the United States, shall be vested in one supreme Court, and in such inferior courts as the Congress may from time to time ordain and establish. The Judges, both of the supreme and inferior courts, shall hold their Offices during good behaviour, and shall, at stated times, receive for their services a compensation, which shall not be diminished during their continuance in office.

Section 2. (1) The judicial power shall extend to all cases, in law and equity, arising under this Constitution, the laws of the United States, and treaties made, or which shall be made, under their authority; - to all cases affecting Ambassadors, other public Ministers and Consuls; - to all cases of admiralty and maritime jurisdiction; - to controversies to which the United States shall be a party; - to controversies between two or more states; - between a state and citizens of another state; - between citizens of different states; - between citizens of the same state claiming lands under the grants of different states, and between a state, or the citizens thereof, and foreign states, citizens or subjects.

(2) In all cases affecting Ambassadors, other public Ministers and Consuls, and those in which a state shall be a party, the supreme Court shall have original jurisdiction. In all the other cases before mentioned, the supreme Court shall have appellate jurisdiction, both as to law and fact, with such exceptions, and under such regulations as the Congress shall make.

(3) The trial of all crimes, except in cases of impeachment, shall be by jury; and such trial shall be held in the state where the said crimes shall have been committed; but when not committed within any state, the trial shall be at such place or places as the Congress may by law have directed.

Section 3. (1) Treason against the United States, shall consist only in levying war against them, or, in adhering to their enemies, giving them aid and comfort. No person shall be convicted of treason unless on the testimony of two witnesses to the same overt act, or on confession in open Court.

(2) The Congress shall have power to declare the punishment of treason, but no Attainder of Treason shall work corruption of blood, or forfeiture except during the life of the person attainted.

ARTICLE IV

Section 1. Full faith and credit shall be given in each state to the public acts, records, and judicial proceedings of every other state. And the Congress may by general laws prescribe the manner in which such acts, records and proceedings shall be proved, and the effect thereof.

Section 2. (1) The citizens of each state shall be entitled to all privileges and immunities of citizens in the several states.

(2) A person charged in any state with treason, felony, or other crime, who shall flee from justice, and be found in another state, shall on demand of the executive authority of the state from which he fled, be delivered up, to be removed to the state having jurisdiction of the crime.

(3) No person held to service or labor in one state, under the laws thereof, escaping into another, shall, in consequence of any law or regulation therein, be discharged from such service or labor, but shall be delivered up on

claim of the party to whom such service or labor may be due.

Section 3. (1) New states may be admitted by the Congress into this union; but no new state shall be formed or erected within the jurisdiction of any other state; nor any state be formed by the junction of two or more states, or parts of states, without the consent of the legislatures of the states concerned as well as of the Congress.

(2) The Congress shall have power to dispose of and make all needful rules and regulations respecting the territory or other property belonging to the United States; and nothing in this Constitution shall be so construed as to prejudice any claims of the United States, or of any particular state.

Section 4. The United States shall guarantee to every state in this union a Republican form of government, and shall protect each of them against invasion; and on application of the legislature, or of the executive (when the legislature cannot be convened) against domestic violence.

ARTICLE V

The Congress, whenever two-thirds of both Houses shall deem it necessary, shall propose amendments to this Constitution, or, on the application of the legislatures of two-thirds of the several states, shall call a convention for proposing amendments, which, in either case, shall be valid to all intents and purposes, as part of this constitution, when ratified by the legislatures of three-fourths of the several states, or by conventions in three-fourths thereof, as the one or the other mode of ratification may be proposed by the Congress; provided that no amendment which may be made prior to the year one thousand eight hundred and eight shall in any manner affect the first and fourth clauses in the Ninth Section of the first Article; and that no state, without its consent, shall be deprived of its equal suffrage in the Senate.

ARTICLE VI

(1) All debts contracted and engagements entered into, before the adoption of this Constitution shall be as valid against the United States under this Constitution, as under the Confederation.

(2) This Constitution, and the laws of the United States which shall be made in pursuance thereof; and all treaties made, or which shall be made, under the authority of the United States, shall be the supreme law of the land; and the Judges in every state shall be bound thereby, any thing in the Constitution or laws of any state to the contrary notwithstanding.

(3) The Senators and Representatives before mentioned, and the Members of the several State Legislatures, and all executive and judicial Officers, both of the United States and of the several states, shall be bound by oath or affirmation, to support this Constitution; but no religious test shall ever be required as a qualification to any office or public trust under the United States.

ARTICLE VII

The ratification of the Conventions of nine states shall be sufficient for the establishment of this Constitution between the states so ratifying the same.

AMENDMENT I (1791)

Congress shall make no law respecting an establishment of religion, or prohibiting the free exercise thereof; or abridging the freedom of speech, or of the press; or the right of the people peaceably to assemble, and to petition the Government for a redress of grievances.

AMENDMENT II (1791)

A well regulated Militia, being necessary to the security of a free state, the right of the people to keep and bear arms, shall not be infringed.

AMENDMENT III (1791)

No soldier shall, in time of peace be quartered in any house, without the consent of the owner, nor in time of war, but in a manner to be prescribed by law.

AMENDMENT IV (1791)

The right of the people to be secure in their persons, houses, papers, and effects, against unreasonable searches and seizures, shall not be violated, and no warrants shall issue, but upon probable cause, supported by oath or affirmation, and particularly describing the place to be searched, and the persons or things to be seized.

AMENDMENT V (1791)

No person shall be held to answer for a capital, or otherwise infamous crime, unless on a presentment or indictment of a Grand Jury, except in cases arising in the land or naval forces, or in the Militia, when in actual service in time of war or public danger; nor shall any person be subject for the same offense to be twice put in jeopardy of life or limb; nor shall be compelled in any criminal case to be a witness against himself, nor be deprived of life, liberty, or property, without due process of law; nor shall private property be taken for public use, without just compensation.

AMENDMENT VI (1791)

In all criminal prosecutions, the accused shall enjoy the right to a speedy and public trial, by an impartial jury of the state and district wherein the crime shall have been committed, which district shall have been previously ascertained by law, and to be informed of the nature and cause of the accusation; to be confronted with the witnesses against him; to have compulsory process for obtaining witnesses in his favor, and to have the assistance of counsel for his defense.

AMENDMENT VII (1791)

In suits at common law, where the value in controversy shall exceed twenty dollars, the right of trial by jury shall be preserved, and no fact tried by jury, shall be otherwise re-examined in any court of the United States, than according to the rules of the common law.

AMENDMENT VIII (1791)

Excessive bail shall not be required, nor excessive fines imposed, nor cruel and unusual punishments inflicted.

AMENDMENT IX (1791)

The enumeration in the Constitution, of certain rights, shall not be construed to deny or disparage others retained by the people.

AMENDMENT X (1791)

The powers not delegated to the United States by the Constitution, nor prohibited by it to the States, are reserved to the States respectively, or to the people.

AMENDMENT XI (1798)

The judicial power of the United States shall not be construed to extend to any suit in law or equity, commenced or prosecuted against one of the United States by citizens of another state, or by citizens or subjects of any foreign state.

AMENDMENT XII (1804)

The Electors shall meet in their respective states and vote by ballot for President and Vice-President, one of whom, at least, shall not be an inhabitant of the same state with themselves; they shall name in their ballots the person voted for as President, and in distinct ballots the person voted for as Vice-President, and they shall make distinct lists of all persons voted for as President, and of all persons voted for as Vice-President, and of the number of votes for each, which lists they shall sign and certify, and transmit sealed to the seat of the government of the United States, directed to the President of the Senate; - the President of the Senate shall, in the presence of the Senate and House of Representatives, open all the certificates and the votes shall then be counted; - the person having the greatest number of votes for President, shall be the President, if such number be a majority of the whole number of electors appointed; and if no person have such majority, then from the persons having the highest numbers not exceeding three on the list of those voted for as President, the House of Representatives shall choose immediately, by ballot, the President. But in choosing the President, the votes shall be taken by states, the representation from each state having one vote; a quorum for this purpose shall consist of a member or members from two-thirds of the states, and a majority of all the states shall be necessary to a choice. And if the House of Representatives shall not choose a President whenever the right of choice shall devolve upon them before the fourth day of March next following, then the Vice-President shall act as President, as in the case of the death or other constitutional disability of the President. - The person having the greatest number of votes as Vice-President, shall be the Vice-President, if such number be a majority of the whole number of Electors appointed, and if no person have a majority, then from the two highest numbers on the list, the Senate shall choose the Vice-President; a quorum for the purpose shall consist of two-thirds of the whole number of Senators, and a majority of the whole number shall be necessary to a choice. But no person constitutionally ineligible to the office of President shall be eligible to that of Vice-President of the United States.

AMENDMENT XIII (1865)

Section 1. Neither slavery nor involuntary servitude, except as a punishment for crime whereof the party shall have been duly convicted, shall exist within the United States, or any place subject to their jurisdiction.

Section 2. Congress shall have power to enforce this article by appropriate legislation.

AMENDMENT XIV (1868)

Section 1. All persons born or naturalized in the United States, and subject to the jurisdiction thereof, are citizens of the United States and of the state wherein they reside. No state shall make or enforce any law which shall abridge the privileges or immunities of citizens of the United States; nor shall any state deprive any person of life, liberty, or property, without due process of law; nor deny to any person within its jurisdiction the equal protection of the laws.

Section 2. Representatives shall be apportioned among the several states according to their respective numbers, counting the whole number of persons in each State excluding Indians not taxed. But when the right to vote at any election for the choice of electors for President and Vice President of the United States, Representatives in Congress, the Executive and Judicial officers of a state, or the members of the Legislature thereof, is denied to any of the male inhabitants of such state, being twenty-one years of age, and citizens of the United States, or in any way abridged, except for participation in rebellion, or other crime, the basis of representation therein shall be reduced in the proportion which the number of such male citizens shall bear to the whole number of male citizens twenty-one years of age in such state.

Section 3. No person shall be a Senator or Representative in Congress, or elector of President and Vice President, or hold any office, civil or military, under the United States, or under any state, who having previously taken an oath, as a member of Congress, or as an officer of the United States, or as a member of any state legislature, or as an executive or judicial officer of any state, to support the Constitution of the United States, shall have engaged in insurrection or rebellion against the same, or given aid or comfort to the enemies thereof. But Congress may by a vote of two-thirds of each House, remove such disability.

Section 4. The validity of the public debt of the United States, authorized by law, including debts incurred for payment of pensions and bounties for services in suppressing insurrection or rebellion, shall not be questioned. But neither the United States nor any state shall assume or pay any debt or obligation incurred in aid of insurrection or rebellion against the United States, or any claim for the loss or emancipation of any slave; but all such debts, obligations and claims shall be held illegal and void.

Section 5. The Congress shall have power to enforce, by appropriate legislation, the provisions of this article.

AMENDMENT XV (1870)

Section 1. The right of citizens of the United States to vote shall not be denied or abridged by the United States or by any state on account of race, color, or previous condition of servitude.

Section 2. The Congress shall have power to enforce this article by appropriate legislation.

AMENDMENT XVI (1913)

The Congress shall have power to lay and collect taxes on incomes, from whatever source derived, without apportionment among the several states, and without regard to any census or enumeration.

AMENDMENT XVII (1913)

(1) The Senate of the United States shall be composed of two Senators from each state, elected by the people thereof, for six years; and each Senator shall have one vote. The electors in each State shall have the qualifications requisite for electors of the most numerous branch of the state legislatures.

(2) When vacancies happen in the representation of any state in the Senate, the executive authority of such state shall issue writs of election to fill such vacancies: *provided*, that the legislature of any state may empower the executive thereof to make temporary appointments until the people fill the vacancies by election as the legislature may direct.

(3) This amendment shall not be so construed as to affect the election or term of any Senator chosen before it becomes valid as part of the Constitution.

AMENDMENT XVIII (1919)

Section 1. After one year from the ratification of this article the manufacture, sale, or transportation of intoxicating liquors within, the importation thereof into, or the exportation thereof from the United States and all territory subject to the jurisdiction thereof for beverage purposes is hereby prohibited.

Section 2. The Congress and the several states shall have concurrent power to enforce this article by appropriate legislation.

Section 3. This article shall be inoperative unless it shall have been ratified as an amendment to the Constitution by the legislatures of the several states, as provided in the Constitution, within seven years from the date of the submission hereof to the states by the Congress.

AMENDMENT XIX (1920)

(1) The right of citizens of the United States to vote shall not be denied or abridged by the United States or by any state on account of sex.

(2) Congress shall have power to enforce this article by appropriate legislation.

AMENDMENT XX (1933)

Section 1. The terms of the President and Vice President shall end at noon on the 20th day of January, and the terms of Senators and Representatives at noon on the 3d day of January, of the years in which such terms would have ended if this article had not been ratified; and the terms of their successors shall then begin.

Section 2. The Congress shall assemble at least once in every year, and such meeting shall begin at noon on the 3d day of January, unless they shall by law appoint a different day.

Section 3. If, at the time fixed for the beginning of the term of the President, the President elect shall have died, the Vice President elect shall become President. If the President shall not have been chosen before the time fixed for the beginning of his term, or if the President elect shall have failed to qualify, then the Vice President elect shall act as President until a President shall have qualified; and the Congress may by law provide for the case wherein neither a President elect nor a Vice President elect shall have qualified, declaring who shall then act as President, or the manner in which one who is to act shall be selected, and such person shall act accordingly until a President or Vice President shall have qualified.

Section 4. The Congress may by law provide for the case of the death of any of the persons from whom the House of Representatives may choose a President whenever the right of choice shall have devolved upon them, and for the case of the death of any of the persons from whom the Senate may choose a Vice President whenever the right of choice shall have devolved upon them.

Section 5. Sections 1 and 2 shall take effect on the 15th day of October following the ratification of this article.

Section 6. This article shall be inoperative unless it shall have been ratified as an amendment to the Constitution by the legislatures of three-fourths of the several states within seven years from the date of its submission.

AMENDMENT XXI (1933)

Section 1. The eighteenth article of amendment to the Constitution of the United States is hereby repealed.

Section 2. The transportation or importation into any state, territory, or possession of the United States for delivery or use therein of intoxicating liquors, in violation of the laws thereof, is hereby prohibited.

Section 3. This article shall be inoperative unless it shall have been ratified as an amendment to the Constitution by conventions in the several states, as provided in the Constitution, within seven years from the date of the submission hereof to the states by the Congress.

AMENDMENT XXII (1951)

Section 1. No person shall be elected to the office of the President more than twice, and no person who has held the office of President, or acted as President, for more than two years of a term to which some other person was elected President shall be elected to the office of President more than once. But this Article shall not apply to any person holding the office of President when this Article was proposed by the Congress, and shall not prevent any person who may be holding the office of President, or acting as President, during the term within which this Article becomes operative from holding the office of President or acting as President during the remainder of such term.

Section 2. This article shall be inoperative unless it shall have been ratified as an amendment to the Constitution by the legislatures of three-fourths of the several states within seven years from the date of its submission to the states by the Congress.

AMENDMENT XXIII (1961)

Section 1. The District constituting the seat of Government of the United States shall appoint in such manner as the Congress may direct:

A number of electors of President and Vice President equal to the whole number of Senators and Representatives in Congress to which the District would be entitled if it were a state, but in no event more than the least populous state; they shall be in addition to those appointed by the states, but they shall be considered, for the purposes of the election of President and Vice President, to be electors appointed by a state; and they shall meet in the District and perform such duties as provided by the twelfth article of amendment.

Section 2. The Congress shall have power to enforce this article by appropriate legislation.

AMENDMENT XXIV (1964)

Section 1. The right of citizens of the United States to vote in any primary or other election for President or Vice President, for electors for President or Vice President, or for Senator or Representative in Congress, shall not be denied or abridged by the United States, or any state by reason of failure to pay any poll tax or other tax.

Section 2. The Congress shall have power to enforce this article by appropriate legislation.

AMENDMENT XXV (1967)

Section 1. In case of the removal of the President from office or of his death or resignation, the Vice President shall become President.

Section 2. Whenever there is a vacancy in the office of the Vice President, the President shall nominate a Vice President who shall take office upon confirmation by a majority vote of both Houses of Congress.

Section 3. Whenever the President transmits to the President pro tempore of the Senate and the Speaker of the House of Representatives his written declaration that he is unable to discharge the powers and duties of his office, and until he transmits to them a written declaration to the contrary, such powers and duties shall be discharged by the Vice President as Acting President.

Section 4. Whenever the Vice President and a majority of either the principal officers of the executive departments or of such other body as Congress may by law provide, transmit to the President pro tempore of the Senate and the Speaker of the House of Representatives their written declaration that the President is unable to discharge the powers and duties of his office, the Vice President shall immediately assume the powers and duties of the office as Acting President.

Thereafter, when the President transmits to the President pro tempore of the Senate and the Speaker of the House of Representatives his written declaration that no inability exists, he shall resume the powers and duties of his office unless the Vice President and a majority of either the principal officers of the executive department or of such

other body as Congress may by law provide, transmit
within four days to the President pro tempore of the Senate and the Speaker of the House of Representatives their
written declaration and the President is unable to discharge the powers and duties of his office. Thereupon
Congress shall decide the issue, assembling within forty-
eight hours for that purpose if not in session. If the Congress, within twenty-one days after receipt of the latter
written declaration, or, if Congress is not in session, within twenty-one days after Congress is required to assemble,
determines by two-thirds vote of both Houses that the
President is unable to discharge the power and duties of
his office, the Vice President shall continue to discharge
the same as Acting President; otherwise, the President
shall resume the powers and duties of his office.

AMENDMENT XXVI (1971)

Section 1. The right of citizens of the United States, who
are eighteen years of age or older, to vote shall not be denied or abridged by the United States or by any state on
account of age.

Section 2. The Congress shall have power to enforce this
article by appropriate legislation.

AMENDMENT XXVII (1992)

No law, varying the compensation for the services of the
Senators and Representatives, shall take effect, until an
election of Representatives shall have intervened.

BIBLIOGRAPHY

Alcorn, Randy C. *Is Rescuing Right? Breaking the Law to Save the Unborn.* Downers Grove, IL: InterVarsity Press, 1990.

Allison, Loraine. *Finding Peace After Abortion.* St. Meinrad, IN: Abbey Press, 1990.

Anderson, Richard. *Abortion Pro & Con.* Los Angeles, CA: Right to Life League, 1977.

Baird, Robert M. and Stuart E. Rosenbaum, Editors. *The Ethics of Abortion: The Continuing Debate.* Buffalo, NY: Prometheus Books, 1989.

Baker, Don. *Beyond Choice: The Abortion Story No One Is Telling.* Portland, OR: Multnomah Press, 1985.

Banks, Bill and Sue Banks. *Ministering to Abortion's Aftermath.* Kirkwood, MO: Impact Books, 1982.

Barry, Robert L. *Medical Ethics: Essays on Abortion and Euthanasia.* Billings, MT: Peter Lang Publications, 1989.

Baulieu, Etienne-Emile and Mort Rosenblum. *The "Abortion Pill": RU-486, A Woman's Choice.* New York, NY: Simon & Schuster, 1991.

Batchelor, Edward, Jr., Editor. *Abortion: The Moral Issues.* New York, NY: Pilgrim Press, 1982.

Berger, G. and W. Brenner, Editors. *Second Trimester Abortion.* Kluwer, N.V.: Kluwer Academic Publishers, 1981.

Bonavoglia, Angela, Editor. *The Choices We Made: 25 Women and Men Speak Out About Abortion.* New York, NY: Random House, 1991.

Bondesor, William B. and H. Tristram Engelhardt. *Abortion and the Status of the Fetus.* Kluwer, N.V.: Kluwer Academic Publishers, 1983.

Braun, Eric A. and LauraLee Gaudio. *Living with Your Choice: An Inner Healing for Abortion.* Sea Cliff, NY: Purelight, 1990.

Briscoe, Clarence C. *Abortion: The Emotional Issue.* Pittsburgh, PA: Dorrance Publishing Co., 1984.

Browder, Clifford. *The Wickedest Woman in New York: Madame Restelle, The Abortionist.* Hamden, CT: Archon Books, 1988.

Brown, Harold O.J. *The Bible on Abortion.* Minneapolis, MN: Free Church Publications, 1977.

Butler, J. Douglas and David F. Walbert, Editors. *Abortion, Medicine and the Law.* New York, NY: Facts on File, 1986.

Callahan, Sidney and Daniel Callahan. *Abortion: Understanding Differences.* New York, NY: Plenum Press, 1984.

Cohen, M., et al., Editors. *Rights and Wrongs of Abortion.* Princeton, NJ: Princeton University Press, 1974.

Condit, Celeste Michelle. *Decoding Abortion Rhetoric: Communicating Social Change.* Chicago: University of Illinois Press, 1990.

Connery, John. *Abortion: The Development of the Roman Catholic Perspective.* Chicago, IL: Loyola University Press, 1977.

Corsaro, Maria and Carole Korzeniowsky. *A Woman's Guide to Safe Abortion.* New York, NY: Holt, Rinehart & Winston, 1983.

Costa, Maria. *Abortion: A Reference Handbook.* Santa Barbara, CA: ABC-CLIO, 1991.

Coughlan, Michael J. *The Vatican, the Law and the Human Embryo.* Iowa City, IA: University of Iowa Press, 1990.

Cozic, Charles and Tracey Tipp, Editors. *Abortion: Opposing Viewpoints.* San Diego, CA: Greenhaven Press, 1991.

Cunningham, Paige C., et al., Editors. *Abortion and the Constitution: Reversing Roe v. Wade Through the Courts.* Washington, DC: Georgetown University Press, 1987.

Curtzinger, G. *Abortion, Person as Thing.* Mansfield, TX: Latitudes Press, 1988.

Davis, John J. *Abortion and the Christian.* Phillipsburg, NJ: Presbyterian & Reformed Publishing Co., 1984.

Devereux, George. *A Study of Abortion in Primitive So-cieties.* Madison, CT: International Universities Press, 1976.

Doerr, Edd and James W. Prescott, Editors. *Abortion Rights and Fetal "Personhood."* Long Beach, CA: Centerline Press, 1990.

Emmens, Carol A. *The Abortion Controversy.* New York, NY: Julian Messner, 1987.

Erdahl, Lowell O. *Pro-Life, Pro-Peace: Life Affirming Alternatives to Abortion, War, Mercy Killing, and the Death Penalty.* Minneapolis, MN: Augsburg Fortress Publishers, 1986.

Faux, Marian. *Crusaders: Voices From the Abortion Front.* Secausus, NJ: Carol Pub. Group, 1990.

Faux, Marion. *Roe v. Wade: The Story of the Landmark Supreme Court Decision That Made Abortion Legal.* New York, NY: Macmillan, 1988.

Feinberg, Joel, Editor. *The Problem of Abortion.* Belmont, CA: Wadsworth Publishing Co., 1984.

Ferraro, Barbara, and Patricia Hussey, with Jane O'Reilly. *No Turning Back: Two Nuns' Battle With the Vatican over Women's Right to Choose.* New York, NY: Poseidon Press, 1990.

Flanders, Carl N. *Abortion.* New York, NY: Facts on File, 1991.

Forelle, Helen. *If Men Got Pregnant, Abortion Would be a Sacrament.* Sioux Falls, SD: Tesseract Publications, 1991.

Fowler, Paul. *Abortion: Toward an Evangelical Consensus.* Portland, OR: Multnomah Press, 1987.

Francke, Linda Bird. *The Ambivalence of Abortion.* New York, NY: Random House, 1978.

Francome, Colin. *Abortion Freedom: A Worldwide Movement.* New York, NY: Unwin Hyman, 1984.

Gardner, Joy. *A Difficult Decision: A Compassionate Book About Abortion.* Trumansburg, NY: Crossing Press, 1986.

Garfield, Jay L. and Patricia Hennessey, Editors. *Abortion: Moral and Legal Perspectives.* Amherst, MA: University of Massachusetts Press, 1985.

Gaylor, Anne N. *Abortion is a Blessing.* New York, NY: Psychological Dimensions, 1976.

Ginsburg, Faye D. *Contested Lives: The Abortion Debate in an American Community.* Berkeley: University of California Press, 1989.

Glessner, Thomas A. *Achieving an Abortion-Free America by 2001.* Portland, OR: Multnomah Press, 1990.

Goldstein, Robert D. *Mother-Love and Abortion: A Legal Interpretation.* Berkeley, CA: University of California Press, 1988.

Grady, John L. *Abortion: Yes or No?* Rockford, IL: TAN Books Pubs., 1968.

Grenier-Sweet, Gail, Editor. *Pro-Life Feminism: Different Voices.* Lewiston, NY: Life Cycle Books, 1985.

Hall, Robert E., Editor. *Abortion in a Changing World.* NY: Columbia University Press, 1970.

Harris, Harry. *Prenatal Diagnosis and Selective Abortion.* Cambridge, MA: Harvard University Press, 1975.

Harrison, Beverly Wildung. *Our Right to Choose: Toward a New Ethic of Abortion.* Boston: Beacon Press, 1983.

Harrison, Maureen, and Steve Gilbert. *Landmark Decisions of the United States Supreme Court, Vol. I.* Beverly Hills, CA: Excellent Books, 1991.

Hern, Warren M. *Abortion Practice.* Boulder, CO: Alpenglo Graphics, 1990.

Hern, Warren M. *Abortion Services Handbook.* Durant, OK: Creative Informatics, 1978.

Hertz, Sue. *Caught in the Crossfire: A Year on Abortion's Front Line.* New York, NY: Prentice Hall, 1991.

Horan, Dennis J., Edward R. Grant and Paige C. Cunningham, Editors. *Abortion and the Constitution: Reversing Roe v. Wade Through the Courts.* Washington, DC: Georgetown University Press, 1987.

Howe, Louise K. *Moments on Maple Avenue: The Reality of Abortion.* New York, NY: Warner Books, 1986.

Ide, Arthur F. *Abortion Handbook: History, Clinical Practice and Psychology of Abortion.* Las Colinas, TX: Liberal Press, 1987.

Imber, Jonathan B. *Abortion and the Private Practice of Medicine.* New Haven, CT: Yale University Press, 1986.

Joyce, Robert and Mary R. Joyce. *Let's Be Born: The Inhumanity of Abortion.* Chicago, IL: Franciscan Herald Press, 1976.

Jung, Patricia Beattie and Thomas A. Shannon, Editors. *Abortion and Catholicism: The American Debate.* New York, NY: Crossroad, 1988.

Justus, Adalu. *Dear Mommy, Please Don't Kill Me.* Hesperia, CA: Silo Pubs., 1986.

Keemer, Edgar B. *Confessions of a Pro-Life Abortionist.* Detroit, MI: Vinco Press, 1980.

Keirse, M. and Bennebroek J. Gravenhorst, Editors. *Second Trimester Pregnancy Termination.* Kluwer, N.V.: Kluwer Academic Publishers, 1982.

Kenyon, Edwin. *The Dilemma of Abortion.* Winchester, MA: Faber & Faber, 1986.

Kerr, Fred W. *Ninety Days for Life: The Jailhouse Journal of "Operation Rescue" Internee, Fred W. Kerr.* Hannibal, MO: Hannibal Books, 1989.

Koerbel, Pam. *Does Anyone Else Feel Like I Do?* New York, NY: Doubleday, 1990.

Kogan, Barry S., Editor. *A Time to be Born and a Time to Die: The Ethics of Choice.* Hawthorne, NY: Aldine de Gruyter, 1991.

Krason, Stephen M. *Abortion: Politics, Morality, and the Constitution: A Critical Study of Roe v., Wade and Doe v. Bolton and a Basis for Change.* Lanham, MD: University Press of America, 1984.

Lader, Lawrence. *Abortion.* New York, NY: Macmillan, 1966.

Lader, Lawrence. *RU-486: The Pill That Could End the Abortion Wars and Why American Women Don't Have It.* New York, NY: Addison-Wesley, 1991.

Lee, Nancy H. *Search for an Abortionist.* Chicago: University of Chicago Press, 1969.

Legge, Jerome S., Jr. *Abortion Policy: An Evaluation of the Consequences for Maternal and Infant Health.* Albany, NY: State University of New York Press, 1985.

Luker, Kristin. *Abortion and the Politics of Motherhood.* Berkeley: University of California Press, 1984.

Luker, Kristin. *Taking Chances: Abortion and the Decision Not to Contracept.* Berkeley: University of California Press, 1975.

Lunneborg, Patricia W. *A Positive Decision.* New York, NY: Bergin & Garvey, 1992.

McCarthy, John F. *In Defense of Human Life.* Houston, TX: Lumen Christi Press, 1970.

McCartney, James J. *Unborn Persons: Pope John Paul II and the Abortion Debate.* New York, NY: Peter Lang Publishing, 1988.

McDonnell, Kathleen. *Not An Easy Choice: A Feminist Re-examines Abortion.* Boston: South End Press, 1984.

Mall, David. *In Good Conscience: Abortion and Moral Necessity.* Columbus, OH: Kairos Books, 1982.

Mannion, Michael T. *Abortion and Healing: A Cry to Be Whole.* Kansas City, MO: Sheed & Ward, 1986.

Melton, Gary B., Editor. *Adolescent Abortion: Psychological and Legal Issues.* Lincoln, NE: University of Nebraska Press, 1986.

Meyers, David W. *The Human Body and the Law.* Palo Alto: Stanford University Press, 1991.

Miley, LaVerne. *Abortion: Right or Wrong?* Nashville, TN: Randall House Publications, 1981.

Mohr, James C. *Abortion in America: The Origins and Evolution of National Policy, 1800-1900.* New York, NY: Oxford University Press, 1978.

Muldoon, Maureen, Editor. *Abortion: An Annotated Indexed Bibliography.* Lewiston, NY: Edwin Mellen Press, 1980.

Nathanson, Sue. *Soul Crisis: One Woman's Journey Through Abortion to Renewal.* New York, NY: New American Library, 1989.

National Issues Forum Staff. *The Battle Over Abortion: Seeking Common Ground in a Divided Nation.* Dubuque, IA: Kendall-Hunt Publishing Co., 1990.

Newman, Sidney H., et al., Editors. *Abortion, Obtained and Denied: Research Aproaches.* New York, NY: Population Council, 1971.

Noonan, John T., Jr. *A Private Choice: Abortion in America in the Seventies.* New York, NY: Free Press, 1979.

Norrie, Kenneth M. *Family Planning and the Law. Santa Cruz, CA: Gower Publishing Co., 1991.*

Odell, Catherine and William Odell. *The First Human Right: A Pro-Life Primer.* Huntington, IN: Our Sunday Visitor, 1983.

Paige, Connie. *The Right to Lifers: Who They Are, How They Operate, Where They Get Their Money.* New York, NY: Summit Books, 1983.

Pastuszek, Eric J. *Is the Fetus Human?* Avon, NJ: Magnificat Press, 1991.

Podell, Janet, Editor. *Abortion.* New York, NY: H.W. Wilson Co., 1990.

Powell, John. *Abortion: The Silent Holocaust.* Allen, TX: Tabor Publishing, 1981.

Reardon, David C. *Aborted Women: Silent No More.* Gaithersburg, MD: Human Life International, 1987.

Reisser, Teri K. and Paul Reisser. *Help for Post-Abortion Women.* Grand Rapids, MI: Zondervan Pub. House, 1989.

Reynolds, Brenda M. *Human Abortion: Guide for Medicine, Science and Research.* Washington, DC: ABBE Publishers Association, 1984.

Rice, Charles E. *Beyond Abortion: The Origin and Future of the Secular State.* Chicago, IL: Franciscan Herald Press, 1978.

Rodman, Hyman, et al. *The Abortion Question.* New York, NY: Columbia University Press, 1990.

Rodman, Hyman and Susan H. Lewis. *The Sexual Rights of Adolescents: Competence, Vulnerability, and Parental Control.* New York, NY: Columbia University Press, 1988.

Rosenblatt, Roger. *Life Itself: Abortion in the American Mind.* New York, NY: Random House, 1992.

Saltenberger, Ann. *Every Woman Has a Right to Know the Dangers of Legal Abortion.* Garrisonville, VA: Air-Plus Enterprises, 1983.

Sarvis, Betty and Hyman Rodman. *The Abortion Controversy.* New York, NY: Columbia University Press, 1974.

Sass, Lauren R., Editor. *Abortion: Freedom of Choice and the Right to Life.* New York, NY: Facts on File, 1978.

Scheidler, Joseph M. *Closed: 99 Ways to Stop Abortion.* Westchester, IL: Crossway Books, 1985.

Siegel, Mark A., Nancy R. Jacobs, and Patricia Von Brook, Editors. *Abortion: An Eternal Social and Moral Issue.* Wylie, TX: Information Plus, 1990.

Skolnick, Gary E. *Abortion: Index of Modern Information with Bibliography.* Washington, DC: ABBE Publishers Association, 1988.

Skowronski, Marjory. *Abortion and Alternatives.* Millbrae, CA: Les Femmes Publishers, 1977.

Sloan, Carole M. *Love, Abortion and Adoption of Carole Lovelee Williams.* Washington, DC: ABBE Publishers Association, 1988.

Sloan, Irving J. The Law Governing Abortion, Contraception and Sterilization. New York, NY: Oceana Publications, 1988.

Sloan, R. Bruce and Diana F. Horvitz. *A General Guide to Abortion.* Chicago, IL: Nelson-Hall, 1973.

Speckhard, Anne. *Psycho-Social Stress Following Abortion.* Kansas City, MO: Sheed & Ward, 1987.

Sproul, R.C. *Abortion: A Rational Look at an Emotional Issue.* Colorado Springs, CO: NavPress, 1990.

Steiner, Gilbert Y., Editor. *The Abortion Dispute and the American System.* Washington, DC: Brookings Institution, 1983.

Steinhoff, Patricia G. and Milton Diamond. *Abortion Politics: The Hawaii Experience.* Honolulu, HI: University of Hawaii Press, 1977.

Storer, Horatio R. and Franklin F. Heard. *Criminal Abortion.* Salem, NH: Ayer Co. Publishers, 1974.

Summerhill, Louise. *The Story of Birthright: The Alternative to Abortion.* Libertyville, IL: Prow Books, 1973.

Szumski, Bonnie, Editor. *Abortion: Opposing Viewpoints.* St. Paul, MN: Greenhaven Press, 1986.

Terkel, Susan Neiburg. *Abortion: Facing the Issues.* New York, NY: Watts, 1988.

Tickle, Phyllis, Editor. *Confessing Conscience: Churched Women on Abortion.* Nashville, TN: Abingdon Press, 1990.

Tooley, Michael. *Abortion and Infanticide. New York, NY: Oxford University Press, 1986.*

Tribe, Laurence H. *Abortion: The Clash of Absolutes.* New York, NY: Norton, 1990.

Wardle, Lynn D. *The Abortion Privacy Doctrine: A Compendium and Critique of Federal Abortion Cases.* Buffalo, NY: W.S. Hein & Co., 1980.

Weinberg, Roy D. *Family Planning and the Law.* Dobbs Ferry, NY: Oceana Publications, 1979.

Welton, K.B. *Abortion is Not a Sin: A New-Age Look at an Age-Old Problem.* Dana Point, CA: Pandit Press, 1988.

Wennberg, Robert. *Life in the Balance: Exploring the Abortion Controversy. Grand Rapids, MI: William B. Eerdmans Publishing Co., 1985.*

Whitney, Catherine. *Whole Life? A Balanced, Comprehensive View of Abortion From Its Historical Context to the Current Debate.* New York, NY: W. Morrow, 1991.

Wilt, Judith. *Abortion, Choice, and Contemporary Fiction: The Armageddon of the Maternal Instinct.* Chicago: University of Chicago Press, 1990.

Winden, Lori Van. *The Case Against Abortion: A Logical Argument for Life.* Ligouri, MO: Liguori Publications, 1988.

INDEX

EXCELLENT BOOKS ORDER FORM

(Please xerox this form so it will be available to other readers.)

Please send

_____ copy(ies) of ABORTION DECISIONS: THE 1970's
_____ copy(ies) of ABORTION DECISIONS: THE 1980's
_____ copy(ies) of ABORTION DECISIONS: THE 1990's
_____ copy(ies) of LANDMARK DECISIONS
_____ copy(ies) of LANDMARK DECISIONS II
_____ copy(ies) of LANDMARK DECISIONS III
_____ copy(ies) of THE ADA HANDBOOK

Name: _____

Address: _____

City: _____ **State:** _____ **Zip:** _____

Price: $15.95 for ABORTION DECISIONS: THE 1970's
         $15.95 for ABORTION DECISIONS: THE 1980's
         $15.95 for ABORTION DECISIONS: THE 1990's
         $14.95 for LANDMARK DECISIONS
         $15.95 for LANDMARK DECISIONS II
         $15.95 for LANDMARK DECISIONS III
         $15.95 for THE ADA HANDBOOK

         Add $1 per book for shipping and handling
         California residents add sales tax

OUR GUARANTEE: Any Excellent Book may be returned at any time for any reason and a full refund will be made.

Mail your check or money order to: Excellent Books, Post Office Box 7121, Beverly Hills, California 90212-7121 or call (310) 275-6945